# A YOUNG PERSON'S
# HISTORY OF
# ISRAEL

# DAVID BAMBERGER

BEHRMAN HOUSE

# A YOUNG PERSON'S HISTORY OF
# ISRAEL

Project Editor: Nick Mandelkern
Book Design: Gilda Hannah
Maps: Kathleen Borowick
Photo Research: Maris Engel
Editorial Assistance: Arthur Kurzweil and Hannah Grad Goodman

Published by Behrman House, Inc.
235 Watchung Ave., West Orange, N.J. 07052
Manufactured in the United States of America

Library of Congress Cataloging in Publication Data

Bamberger, David.
  A young person's history of Israel.
  1. Zionism—History—Juvenile literature. 2. Palestine
—History—Juvenile literature. 3. Israel—History—
Juvenile literature. I. Title.
DS149.B318   1985        956.94'001        84-28215
ISBN 0-87441-393-1


  2 3 4 5 6 7        86 87 88 89 90

*For*

*My son Steven*

**Who, among his wonderful
qualities, was a delightful
traveling companion in Israel**

THANKS . . .

to Jacob Behrman, for asking me to express
my love for Israel in a book

to my parents, Rabbi and Mrs. Bernard J.
Bamberger, who instilled in me a love
for Judaism and first took me to Israel

to Rabbi Morrison David Bial, for his
detailed and enormously useful notes
on my manuscript

to Beth Israel-The West Temple, Cleveland,
Ohio, for its wonderful library

to my mother-in-law, Mrs. Elly Beral, for
adding so much to my family's most recent
visit to Israel by joining us there

and
to my wife Carola, the perfect companion and
colleague, who ultimately deserves the
credit for most of what I accomplish.

DB

# Contents

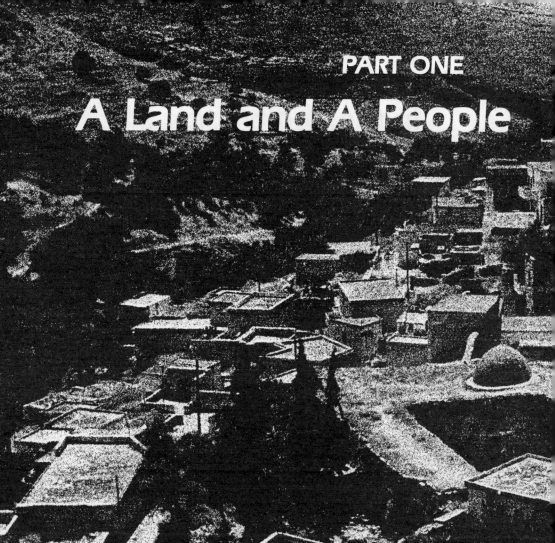

**PART ONE**

# A Land and A People

## Chapter One

# In the Beginning. . . . .

The earth cracked. The bottom of the ancient valley suddenly dropped. The screams of trapped animals and the shrieks of escaping birds were drowned by the thunderous roar of an earthquake.

The land on either side of the valley was pushed and twisted into hills, as if the earth were no more than a piece of paper being crumpled by a giant hand. Molten rock broke through the earth's crust, forming fiery volcanoes.

The geography of the land of Israel was being created.

**A Famous Valley**   The ground came to rest. In time the volcanoes cooled. Water began to flow through the valley that had been formed by the earthquake. From one end of the valley to the other was only eighty miles. The earthquake had left the land so scarred and broken, however, that the water had to twist and turn for a full 200 miles to pass through it.

At the southern end of the valley, the water flowed down to the lowest point on earth, 1305 feet below sea level. There it filled a deep crack in the earth's surface, and formed the Dead Sea.

The river had dropped so far down on its journey to the Dead Sea that it was given a name taken from the Hebrew word, *yarden*—"descending." In English, the word *yarden* became *Jordan*.

**The First Humans**   The great earthquake that created the Jordan River took place a million years ago, when there were no humans on earth. It was 500,000 years later that the Jordan Valley first felt the foot of what we would recognize as a human being.

These early humans were small, and hair covered their bodies. They had no homes. They simply wandered from place to place looking for plants they could eat, or animals they could kill for food and clothing.

This Skylab photo shows how the land of Israel appears from high above the earth's surface. The Dead Sea fills the center of the picture, and above it the Jordan River looks like a dark, narrow ribbon. Mountain ridges on both sides descend sharply into the Jordan Valley.

A closer look at the steep, jagged edge of the Jordan Valley (left). These cliffs, created about a million years ago by powerful earthquakes and volcanic eruptions, are at Qumran, near the Dead Sea.

The Jordan River (below) twists and bends on its way to the Dead Sea, the lowest point on the face of the earth.

**Cave Men** The early humans had to find shelter from the cold. This was easy in the land of Israel, where limestone mountains are filled with caves. The early humans moved into them and became "cave men."

We often think of cave men as the most primitive of humans. Actually, moving to a cave marked an important step for humanity! Earlier people had been wanderers, like other animals. The cave man had a place of his own, where he could live with his family.

He discovered that he truly cared for the members of his family. When those he loved died, he buried them so that they would have a permanent cave of their own.

He began to ask himself where others went after they died, and whether their spirits continued to live. He wondered what made the world work as it did, and how he could gain the support of those forces that seemed to control his life.

**The Birth of Agriculture** For nearly 100,000 years, the life of the cave man continued almost unchanged. He hunted, and ate plants that grew near his cave. When the food supply ran out, he moved to another cave. Then he learned to save the seeds of plants and plant them in the earth. When the seeds sprouted, he tended the young plants. He learned that they needed sun and water.

The plants grew. Agriculture was born.

**The Agricultural Revolution** People learned more and more about plants—how to care for them, and how to grow them for food. These discoveries revolutionized human life.

Now humans could live anywhere that they could grow food. New shelters were built near fertile land. At first these were primitive huts, but later more comfortable structures were built.

Families, and groups of families, built their homes near each other, so that they could help and protect one another. People built houses in the Jordan Valley, near an everflowing spring. Eventually the clusters of houses grew into small towns.

One of the earliest towns still exists. Its name is Jericho.

**Civilization Develops** Jericho grew. Other towns arose. Not everyone chose to live in towns. Some people made their livings as wandering shepherds. Even today their descendants continue the wandering life. They are called "nomads." The Arab nomads are known as Bedouin.

Life in the towns, however, was easier than the world of the nomads, with its constant struggle for survival. Townspeople found, for example, that by heating certain rocks they could get a brown metal that produced far better tools than could be made from stone. Thus, the first copper tools were developed.

People thought more and more about the forces in the universe which they felt, but could not understand or control. They believed that every force of nature was controlled by a different god. Certain individuals tried to communicate with these gods. They performed ceremonies, tried to please gods, and told traditional stories of gods and goddesses.

Organized religion had begun.

**The World of History** Jericho was founded about 10,000 years ago. People spoke to each other to communicate; but it was another 5000 years before anyone kept a permanent record of

About 10,000 years ago, the residents of Jericho built this tower, probably to store harvested grain. The ability to grow and store food allowed people to live in much larger communities than ever before. These ruins, discovered in our own time under layers of dirt and dust, are from one of the first cities of human history.

what had been said. It was only about 3000 B.C.E. that writing was developed.

At first, writing was mostly a tool for business use. The earliest written documents are lists for merchants, contracts, and other agreements. Eventually, others began to use the new system of notation. Priests wrote down tales of the gods, prayers, and rituals.

When kings began to have records kept of their battles and conquests, the *pre*historic period ended. *Recorded* history had begun.

## SUMMARY

The land of Israel, as we know it, was formed a million years ago by an earthquake that created the Jordan Valley. Human history began half a million years later, with primitive human beings. The growth of civilization was very slow: from toolmaker to cave man, from the development of agriculture to the building of towns (the oldest town in the world is Jericho in the Jordan Valley). Then came the development of more advanced tools and organized religion. Writing was developed only 5000 years ago. The invention of writing marks the end of the prehistoric period and the beginning of recorded history.

## SPECIAL TOPIC

### Choosing Our Future

The earth is billions of years old. The Jordan Valley is a million years old. Human recorded history is a mere 5000 years old. Yet in that brief time, thanks to writing, we have developed more than in the previous 100,000 years. We can modify the environment. Yet, amazingly, we have learned in that comparatively short time how to build bombs that can destroy the earth. We have the power to choose a future for the planet. Never before have we been able to understand so well the words of the Torah:

> I the Lord call heaven and earth to witness against you this day: I have put before you life and death, blessing and curse. Choose life.
> (*Deuteronomy* 30:19)

## Chapter Two

# A Homeland Won and Lost

**B**y the year 2000 B.C.E. the land of Israel was flourishing, inhabited by people known as the Canaanites.

The life of the Canaanites was controlled in many ways by the geography of the country. The hills and valleys created by the great earthquake separated the towns. Each Canaanite tribe lived separately, relying on its own slim resources.

In other lands, great rivers connected the cities. Communities were able to combine their resources and create great empires. For example, the Egyptians used the Nile River to carry materials for magnificent stone palaces and gigantic pyramids. But each isolated Canaanite town just built small shrines of mudbrick.

**The Promised Land**   Centuries passed, but the land of Israel gave no indication that it would ever be an important place. Not very fertile, poor in natural resources, it seemed to offer little to the world.

All this was changed by one man: Abraham.

Abraham was born in the eighteenth century B.C.E., far from Eretz Yisrael. His home was the wealthy city of Ur, located in Mesopotamia near the great Euphrates River.

Abraham did not believe in the pagan gods and goddesses. He believed there was only one God who controlled all the world.

Abraham was the first Jew.

He decided to leave Ur and travel some 750 miles west to settle in the comparatively primitive land of Canaan.

Why did he make this dramatic change in his life? Because, the Torah tells us, God told him to do so. And in Canaan, God made Abraham a great promise, saying:

> Raise your eyes and look out from where you are, to the north
> and south, to the east and west, for I give all the land that you

see to you and your offspring forever. . . . Up, walk about the land, through its length and breadth, for I give it to you.

(*Genesis* 13:14,17)

Abraham was promised a homeland by God! How could such a thing happen? How could he explain what he had experienced? Many of his own people must have thought he was foolish, or even insane.

Today the State of Israel exists because, for 4000 years, the Jewish people have continued to believe in the promise God made to Abraham.

**Slow Steps**  This does not mean that the Hebrew people took control of the land quickly. It was a very long process. The Hebrews had to leave Canaan for Egypt because of a fearful drought. In Egypt they were enslaved for four centuries, then freed under the leadership of Moses. They received the Ten Commandments at Mount Sinai, then wandered in the desert for a generation.

Abraham's journey took him from Mesopotamia, the great center of ancient civilization, to Canaan, the land promised him by God.

The Wanderings of Abraham
about 1800 B.C.E.

On their way to the land of Israel, the ancient Hebrews wandered through the rugged mountains (above) and windswept oases (below) of the Sinai desert.

King David made Jerusalem his capital. The area at the bottom of this picture is still known as the "City of David." The large dome, center, marks the site where King Solomon's Temple once stood.

When they at last returned to Eretz Yisrael in the twelfth century B.C.E., it took them almost a century to conquer the land.

In all, it was 800 years before the Hebrews were united into one nation, and set up a kingdom under the rule of King David.

**David and Solomon** King David is one of the most dramatic figures in Jewish history. His poems and songs created a new tradition in Jewish literature, represented by the beautiful psalms that are part of our Bible and prayerbook. He was a great warrior whose victories built a nation of the loosely joined Hebrew tribes.

And his decision to build a new capital in Jerusalem turned

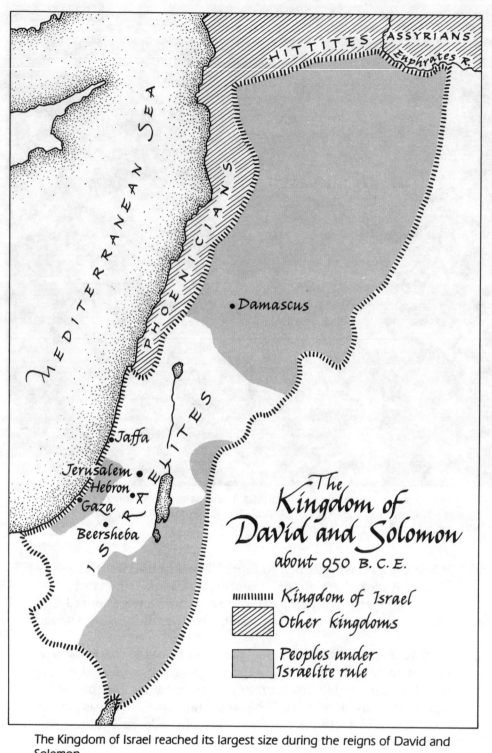

The Kingdom of David and Solomon about 950 B.C.E.

HITTITES ASSYRIANS
Euphrates R.
MEDITERRANEAN SEA
PHOENICIANS
• Damascus
• Jaffa
Jerusalem •
Hebron •
• Gaza
Beersheba •
I S R A E L I T E S

The
Kingdom of
David and Solomon
about 950 B.C.E.

Kingdom of Israel
Other kingdoms
Peoples under
Israelite rule

The Kingdom of Israel reached its largest size during the reigns of David and Solomon.

the hill-town into a city which would one day be holy to three great religions.

David's son, King Solomon, made Jerusalem a city of splendor. He built a beautiful Temple to serve as the central shrine of the Hebrew people. In addition, he made the country into a center of international trade. The land enjoyed peace for many years.

**Destruction . . . and Hope** When Solomon died, his sons battled for the throne. They split the nation into two kingdoms, Israel in the north, Judah in the south. The Kingdom of Israel was destroyed by the Assyrians in 722 B.C.E., the Kingdom of Judah by Babylonia in 586 B.C.E. The Hebrews were sent into exile. It looked as if they would disappear from the pages of history.

This did not happen, even though no other people has ever survived without a homeland. The Jews survive to this day.

How did this happen?

The Jews believed they had a duty to survive. They had been chosen by God to bring His law to the world. As one prophet put it, they were to be "a light to the nations." The prophet Isaiah described the wonderful day when the world would finally learn God's law of justice, truth, and peace, as He had taught it to the Jewish people:

> And they shall beat their swords into plowshares
> And their spears into pruning hooks:
> Nation shall not take up
> Sword against nation;
> They shall never again know war.                    (*Isaiah* 2:4)

Just as important, the Jews knew they still had a homeland. They might be separated from it. They might be exiled from it. But the homeland had been given to them by God. Nothing could ever cancel His promise to Abraham.

**A New Invention** In 516 B.C.E., the Persian King Darius allowed the Jews to return from the Babylonian Exile to Eretz Yisrael. They returned to rebuild their land.

They rebuilt Jerusalem. They planted farms and vineyards. They built a Second Temple. And they built smaller houses of worship throughout the land.

We call this new place of worship the synagogue. In the synagogue, study and prayer replaced sacrifice and offerings.

Wherever they settled Jews built synagogues, their "new invention." These ruins, in Capernaum in northern Israel, date from the second or third century C.E.

Jewish law stated that sacrifices could be offered only at the Temple in Jerusalem. A synagogue could be built anywhere. Synagogues rose throughout the Diaspora, some of them small and simple, some of them large and beautifully decorated. After the Temple was destroyed, the synagogue became the home of Jewish worship throughout the world. It became a place of meeting, study and prayer.

Other religions saw the value of this Jewish institution. The synagogue became the model for Christian churches and Muslim mosques.

**Invasion Follows Invasion** Since Eretz Yisrael lies at the crossroads of important routes from Africa to Asia, the land was not left in peace. Any country that wanted power in the region had to control the land of Israel.

As a result, one invading army followed another.

The Assyrians seized the land in 722 B.C.E. and carried the northern tribes into exile—the Ten Lost Tribes of Israel.

The Babylonians conquered the land in 586 B.C.E., and destroyed the Temple of Solomon.

The Babylonians were conquered by the Persians.

The Persians were defeated by the brilliant Greek general, Alexander the Great.

Alexander died, and his generals fought for control of his empire. Eretz Yisrael fell into the hands of the mad king Antiochus.

**The Maccabees Revolt**  Antiochus tried to force the Jews to accept the Greek religion. Revolt broke out, led by a priest named Mattathias and his son Judah, "the Maccabee."

Antiochus had large forces of trained soldiers, weapons, and even war elephants. Judah Maccabee had a small band of followers who were devoted to the Law of God. That was enough to give him victory.

Judah had an important ally: the land of Israel itself. The twisted hills and valleys, the mountains and caves, the forest and

Kibbutz members put the finishing touches on a menorah, the symbol of Hanukkah. Two thousand years after the Maccabees' victory, the Jewish people have once again established an independent state in their own land.

the desert, all provided places where he and his men could hide. They could reappear just as suddenly, striking the enemy when least expected.

After two years of courageous fighting, Judah and his warriors drove the Greek soldiers out of Jerusalem. For the first time in history, a people had fought a war for freedom of religion.

We still celebrate the victory of the Maccabees with the joyous holiday of Hanukkah.

**A Taste of Independence**  For one hundred years, the descendents of Mattathias ruled an independent Jewish state. Sad to say, although the family produced great soldiers, it produced very poor kings. During the century that the family ruled, they all but wrecked the country.

Finally two princes began to compete for the throne. They realized that their arguments might start a civil war, so they looked for someone to choose between them. They turned to a Roman general who happened to be in the area.

The Roman general's solution was simple. He ignored both princes, and made Eretz Yisrael part of the Roman Empire.

The Jewish people had had only a brief taste of independence. It would be more than 2000 years before the descendants of Abraham would again be masters of their homeland.

## SUMMARY

Abraham received God's promise that his descendents would rule Eretz Yisrael. Under King David and King Solomon, a Hebrew empire was indeed established, with its capital at Jerusalem. Two factors kept Hebrew rule from being permanent. The land of Israel is a crossroads for routes through the Middle East, and one great army after another battled to control the area. Equally important, the rivalries within the Hebrew royal families shattered both the kingdom of David and the much later kingdom created by the victorious Maccabees. Once Rome took control of Eretz Yisrael, Jewish independence was lost for 2000 years.

## Chapter Three

# Eagle, Cross, and Crescent

The eagle ruled Eretz Yisrael.

The eagle was the symbol of the powerful Roman empire, which grew to include Britain, most of Europe, all of North Africa, and the Middle East.

The land promised to Abraham was now just a tiny province of the Roman Empire. It was known to the Romans as "Judea."

**Under the Romans** The emperors in Rome, far from Judea, intended to rule the land fairly. They were sensitive to the Jewish religion. Since Judaism forbids sculptures that might be used as idols, the Romans told their soldiers not to bring carvings of the Roman eagle into the holy city of Jerusalem.

Unfortunately, the governors who were stationed in Judea had other aims. They were hardened soldiers whose goal was to steal as much as they could from a country before they were transferred to other posts. One of them even took gold from the Temple treasury for his personal use. When the Jews protested, thousands were massacred.

**Rebellion** The country exploded in rebellion. Tiny Judea challenged the world's mightiest empire.

The Romans expected to crush the rebellion with ease. They were wrong. The Jewish forces gave the Roman army one of its most difficult challenges. It was four years before the Romans could reach the gates of Jerusalem. They surrounded the city, and still the Jews held them back for five months.

But the Roman army was too powerful to be stopped. On the ninth day of the month of Av in 70 C.E., the Roman battering rams smashed through the walls of Jerusalem. Soon the great Temple was in flames.

One of the many surviving signs of Roman rule, this 2000-year-old aqueduct carried drinking water from town to town. It stands near Caesarea, midway between Haifa and Tel Aviv.

Masada, where Jewish resisters made a last, desperate stand against the Roman Empire.

**On to Masada**   Still the rebellion continued. A group of about 1000 Jews escaped from Jerusalem to a mountain in the desert called Masada. Its steep sides and flat top made it a natural fortress. There the Jews remained safe from the Roman army for three years.

At last the Romans built a huge ramp to the top of Masada. They marched up the ramp and smashed through the defending walls. They were met by solemn silence. The defenders, preferring death to slavery, had taken their own lives.

**Bar Kochba**   Despite this terrible defeat, the Jews still longed for independence. The Romans applied oppressive laws, which only made Jews more eager to be free. Finally the Romans issued their sternest decree: No one was permitted to teach Torah.

Again rebellion broke out, this time led by a dynamic and daring soldier. His followers called him Bar Kochba, "Son of a Star." For three years he led the Jewish resistance. However, the unlimited power of Rome could not be defeated. Bar Kochba was driven from Jerusalem and killed in battle.

**Roman Revenge**   The Romans had paid heavily for their victory; they took cruel revenge. More than half a million Jews were killed or sold as slaves. Anyone who taught Judaism was executed. Jewish settlements were destroyed. Even the country's name was changed. Rome had called the land "Judea"—the Latin name for "Judah." But now it was not to be thought of as the land of the Jews. It was rather to be named after the Philistines, who had disappeared many centuries before.

Judea was now known as "Palestine."

**Roman Defeat**   It appeared that the Romans could rejoice in a great triumph. In fact, they were losing two battles.

They could not win the battle against Judaism. Rabbis risked death to teach the Torah. Other Jews risked death to study, and to practice their religion. Eventually the Romans were forced to change their laws to permit Jewish practices. Jewish schools were built. Synagogues were built. Jewish learning flourished, leading to the creation of the great treasurehouse of Jewish law and knowledge, the Talmud.

At the same time, the Romans were losing their battle against a group of Jews who believed that a rabbi who had been executed in Jerusalem was in reality the son of God. The religion they

The Romans destroyed the Temple in Jerusalem. All that remains are the huge stones of the Western Wall, which to this day hold cherished memories for the Jewish people.

practiced is called "Christianity." Although Christians were arrested and killed, the religion found more and more converts. About 350 years after the death of the man they called Jesus Christ, Christianity became the official religion of the Roman Empire.

**Christian Rule**　Now the rulers of Palestine carried the Christian cross instead of the Roman eagle. The land of Israel was governed by people whose religion was based on Judaism and whose prophet was a Jew.

This did not help the Jews living in Eretz Yisrael. The Christian rulers were fiercely anti-Jewish. Life for the Jewish community was extremely grim. The center of Jewish life gradually shifted to Babylonia, where the Jews enjoyed greater freedom than in Palestine.

**The Muslims**　About the year 600 C.E., an Arab boy came to Palestine on a caravan journey. The boy, Muhammad, was very impressed by what he saw. At his home in Arabia, his fellow

Arabs believed in many gods, and worshipped them with wild revels. In Palestine, one God was worshipped in a respectful way. Drunkenness was part of Arab ceremonies, but Jews and Christians used wine only as part of solemn rituals. Furthermore, Arabs with too many daughters took the unwanted girls and buried them alive. But the people of Israel taught: "You shall not murder."

Based in part on what he saw in Palestine, Muhammad started a new religion which he called "Islam." The Arabs flocked to his ideas and became "Muslims", or followers of Islam.

Muhammad taught that it was good to fight, and even die, to spread his new religion. A fight on behalf of Islam was called a "holy war." Inflamed by this idea, his followers created armies and fought fierce wars. For one hundred years they moved from victory to victory. A century after Muhammad's death, the crescent moon—the symbol of Islam—flew from Spain on the west to India on the east.

Eretz Yisrael was the first stop on the Muslim march. Except for a brief interruption, Muslims ruled the land for nearly 1300 years.

**The Crusades**  The brief interruption was during the time of the Crusades. These were wars launched by the Christians of Europe to try to recapture the land of Jesus from the Muslims.

This period has produced many legends of gallant knights fighting heroic battles. In fact, the knights fought few heroic battles. Several Crusader armies never even reached the Holy Land! And when they did fight, they were anything but gallant. As they marched across Europe, they murdered innocent Jewish men, women and children. After conquering Jerusalem, the Crusaders slaughtered almost every Jew and Muslim in the city.

In time, the Christians were driven away. They left behind crumbling castles, and some fascinating ruins in the city of Acre. Other than that, the land of Palestine was very little changed.

The most important results of the Crusades were in Europe. At that time Europe was a very crude and backward continent, where bathing was a rare sign of culture. The soldiers returned from the Middle East with tales of a glorious world—a world of Persian carpets, flower gardens, and warm seas. The foods they sent home changed the life of Europe. Most popular were the delicacies called in Arabic *sukkar* and *qandi*—sugar and candy! Inspired by the Middle East, European civilization grew.

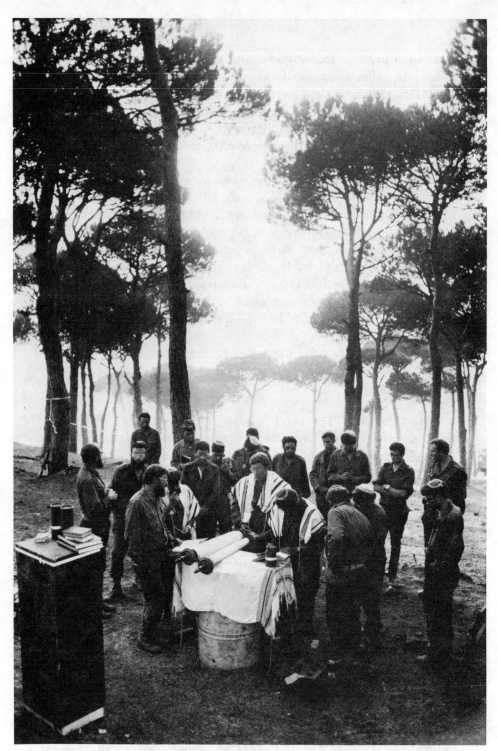

Israeli soldiers praying in a wooded field. "Not by might, nor by power, but by my spirit—says the Lord."

**Peace and Destruction**  With the Christians gone, the land returned to Muslim rule. The next centuries were relatively peaceful. But it was a peace that did not mean happiness. For the land of Israel, it was a peace that meant destruction.

## SUMMARY

The harshness of Roman rule led to two Jewish rebellions. The Jews fought bravely, but in each case were defeated by the huge resources of Rome. Still, Rome could defeat neither Judaism, nor a new religion which sprang from Judaism: Christianity. Christian rule was in turn ended by the Muslims, who defeated the Christians a second time in the Crusades. None of these changes helped either the Jews or the land of Israel. The real strength of the Jews lay in their spiritual values.

## SPECIAL TOPIC

### Our Strongest Weapon

While we must admire the bravery of the Jews who battled the Roman armies, we must also realize that they were eventually defeated. The Jewish people survived because of others who also risked their lives, but whose only weapon was the Torah. These men were the rabbis who heroically insisted on teaching and practicing Judaism in defiance of Roman law.

Today we all know that the State of Israel must have an excellent army to protect itself from its enemies. It must have well trained soldiers and the finest equipment. But nothing in Jewish history suggests that weapons alone will be enough to preserve us. Thousands of years ago the prophet Zechariah told us the key to survival:

Not by might, nor by power, but by My spirit—says the Lord of Hosts.     (*Zechariah* 4:6)

## Chapter Four

# Under Muslim Rule

Land can die. That may seem an odd idea. We think of people dying. Of animals dying. But not land.

Yet land can die as well. Fertile land can turn to sand. Sand can become desert. Sand can blow away, leaving bare rock.

Jews have always known this. The Torah includes laws to protect the land. The land was to be given periods of rest from farming in order to keep it fertile. Even during warfare, it was to be guarded. The Torah orders us not to cut down fruit trees.

**The Conquerors' View** The nations who conquered Eretz Yisrael did not share this concern for the land.

They destroyed trees and plants. The earth that had been held together by the tree roots began to dry out and crumble.

The eroding soil was carried away by wind and rain. It clogged rivers and streams. The water backed up and formed swamps. The swamps became a breeding place for the mosquito that carries the deadly disease, malaria.

**The Arabs** Each new Muslim conqueror brought hope to the Jews in Palestine. Each began to rebuild. Yet each thought of Eretz Yisrael as only a poor corner of a great empire—and soon lost interest in it.

The first Muslim conquerors were Arabs. They regarded Jerusalem as a holy city. According to their tradition, Muhammad was carried from Mecca to Jerusalem on a winged white horse, and landed on the hilltop where Solomon's Temple had once stood.

The Arabs cleared the Temple Mount of all the rubbish that had accumulated there during the years of Christian rule. They uncovered a huge boulder, 58 by 44 feet. Jews believe this stone marks the location of the most sacred part of the Jerusalem Temple, the Holy of Holies. Muslims believe Muhammad's horse leaped from the rock to carry him into the heavens.

The Arabs built an exquisite structure around the sacred stone. Its magnificent golden dome gives it the name, "Dome of the Rock." It is one of the most beautiful buildings in the world.

**The Mamelukes and Ottomans**  The next Muslim rulers came from Egypt. They were called the Mamelukes. Among their constructions was a remarkable bridge which not only still stands (after 700 years), but also supports one of the busiest highways in Israel.

The last Muslims to rule Palestine were the Ottoman Turks. Their rulers, called Sultans, governed from what is now Turkey. Sultan Suleiman the Magnificent built the walls which still surround the Old City of Jerusalem. Mosques were built and redecorated, schools were opened, and water supplies restored.

But these enthusiastic projects were followed by years of neglect. Roads were permitted to crumble. Farm after farm was abandoned. Since Muslims do not drink alcoholic beverages, vineyards were torn up and destroyed.

The land continued to die.

**With the Ottoman Turks**  Through all this, to Jews the country remained what it had been since the time of Abraham: the Promised Land. Even as conditions became worse and worse, Jews continued to live in Palestine, and others returned to live and study there. Most of them survived in poverty, relying on donations sent to them from Jews around the world.

When Spain's large Jewish population was expelled in 1492, many followed the Ottoman Turks into Palestine. They settled in the four cities that were regarded as especially holy. First, of course, was Jerusalem. Second was Hebron, site of the tomb of Abraham, Isaac, Jacob, and their wives Sarah, Rebekah, and Leah. (Jacob's second wife, Rachel, was buried on the road to Bethlehem.) Tiberias, one of the great seats of Jewish learning, was third.

In the 1500s, however, the most creative center of Jewish life was the fourth holy city—Safed.

Safed is beautifully set on a mountaintop overlooking the valley of Jezreel. It is known for its clear air and bright light, and is well-located for trade. It became the focus of the Jewish world, however, because of the great movement that arose there — Jewish mysticism.

The Dome of the Rock, one of the most beautiful buildings in the world, was built by the Arab conquerers of Jerusalem in the seventh century.

Inside the Dome of the Rock is the Rock itself, holy to both Jews and Muslims. According to tradition, Abraham came to this place when God commanded him to offer his son, Isaac, as a sacrifice. Hundreds of years later, King Solomon built his Temple here. And Muslims believe that their prophet, Muhammad, ascended to heaven from this very spot.

**Dreams of Messiah**   The rabbis in Safed were not interested merely in learning for its own sake. They believed that through their work they could transform history.

All Jews prayed for the day when the Temple would be rebuilt in Jerusalem, and the whole Jewish people would return to Eretz Yisrael. They realized that this could not happen through ordinary means. They believed that God would send a savior who would miraculously reestablish the Kingdom of Israel, and would bring the world a new era of peace and justice.

This man would be the Messiah.

The hope for a Messiah has been a strong force throughout Jewish history. Even today some Jews pray that the Messiah will come and rebuild the Temple. Many Jews pray for the "Messianic Age," an era of peace and righteousness throughout the world.

**Isaac Luria**   In periods of oppression, the Jewish yearning for the Messiah became desperate. Some hoped that extraordinary studies and prayers would bring the Messiah. They formed a community in Safed to pursue these studies and prayers.

A leader of the group was Rabbi Isaac Luria, known as ARI ("The Lion"). Many regarded him as a saint with more than human powers. The synagogue in which he prayed remains a holy place to this day.

The ARI died when he was only in his thirties. Yet his personality so inspired his followers that many Jews throughout the world believed that the days of the Messiah were at hand.

**Joseph Karo**   Another rabbi in Safed, Joseph Karo, had a very different life. Exiled from Spain when he was only four, he traveled with his parents to Turkey. He was deeply affected by those who felt that the Messiah would soon arrive.

He also had another concern. With Jews being driven from country to country, religious practices began to differ from region to region. How would Jews know the correct observance? Karo examined all the key Jewish law codes, chose among conflicting opinions, and decided which was the most correct.

He produced a handbook of Jewish practice called the *Shulchan Aruch*, "The Set Table." It became the standard guide for Jewish observance, and is still the basis for Orthodox practice.

**Shabbetai Zevi**   All the talk about the coming of the Messiah created excitement and anticipation throughout the Jewish

A view of Safed, one of Israel's most picturesque towns. Safed still has the look and feel of the sixteenth century, when Jewish mystics and scholars walked its steep, narrow alleyways.

world. In the seventeenth century, a Jew from Turkey claimed that he was the Messiah. His name was Shabbetai Zevi.

He traveled to Egypt, to Palestine, and to major cities elsewhere. He promised to lead all Jews back to Eretz Yisrael. You can tell how desperate many Jews were by their eagerness to believe him. Jews in Europe sold their belongings and waited for his signal to move to the Holy Land. The Jews of Eretz Yisrael, among whom he lived for a time, were ready to hail him as their king.

Yet he proved to be a disappointment. When Shabbetai Zevi returned to Turkey, the sultan had him arrested. The would-be Messiah was offered a choice: conversion to Islam or death. He chose Islam, leaving his Jewish followers in despair.

**Napoleon**   Palestine again affected world history when Napoleon Bonaparte led a French army into Egypt, and then set out to conquer Palestine. He took Jaffa easily; but he was not prepared for the response he received at Acre.

The Ottoman governor had made the city of Acre into a strong fortress. In addition, he had a "secret weapon"—his brilliant adviser, a Jew named Hayyim Farhi. Farhi organized the city's defense magnificently.

Napoleon would prove to be one of Europe's greatest generals, but against the walls of Acre he was helpless. After three months of siege, in which he lost about 3000 soldiers, he left Palestine in defeat.

**The Land Fades**   Despite these moments of crisis, the fact remains that Eretz Yisrael was not an important part of the Ottoman empire. Like the Arabs and Mamelukes, the Ottomans lost interest in the Holy Land.

In the 1800s, while Europe and America were growing rapidly, the Middle East declined. The Ottoman Empire decayed. The land of Israel fell into ruin. Some Jews and Christians clung

During Ottoman rule, much of the land of Israel fell into neglect. Cactus plants grew where fruit trees once bloomed. But about one hundred years ago, Jewish pioneers began coming to the land, bringing modern agricultural techniques and a fierce determination to make the desert bloom once again. Their sons and daughters, born to a harsh life in difficult surroundings, became known as Sabras—a name taken from the fruit of this cactus. There is an Israeli saying: Like the sabra fruit, native-born Israelis are tough on the outside, but tender within.

to their holy sites, living among equally poor and dejected Arabs. The land of milk and honey had become a neglected, filthy place, filled with hunger and disease.

Most people believed that the land was dead. A few realized that it was just waiting to be reborn.

## SUMMARY

Three groups of Muslims have ruled Eretz Yisrael: the Arabs, the Mamelukes, and the Ottoman Turks. Each began its control over the Holy Land with efforts at rebuilding, then lost interest, and permitted the land to decay. Misery and persecution throughout the Jewish world led Jews to hope for salvation through the coming of the Messiah. Some notable rabbis—especially Isaac Luria and Joseph Karo — settled in Safed, hoping that their prayers would encourage God to send the Messiah. A false Messiah, Shabbetai Zevi, attracted much attention. None of this changed the slow deterioration of the country into a place of filth, hunger, and disease.

## SPECIAL TOPIC

### Muslims and Arabs

In order to understand current events in the Middle East, it is necessary to know the difference between the terms "Muslim" and "Arab."

A **Muslim** is "a person who follows the religion of Islam." There are large communities of Muslims throughout Africa and Asia, including the Middle East, Indonesia, and Russia.

An **Arab** is "a person whose ancestors came from Arabia." Most Arabs live in the Middle East in countries like Saudi Arabia, Jordan, and Syria. Most Arabs are Muslims—but there are also Arab Christians and Druses.

The first Muslims who conquered Palestine were Arabs. They were defeated in 1250 by Muslims who were not Arabs, the Mamelukes. The Mamelukes were defeated by other non-Arab Muslims, the Ottoman Turks.

This means that, while Muslims ruled Palestine for many centuries, the Arabs have not controlled the country for more than 700 years.

# PART TWO

# Early Zionism

## Chapter Five

# The Birth of a Dream

The 1800s: Telegraph wires carrying messages around the world. Steamships crossing the ocean. Railroad trains roaring on ribbons of steel. Growing cities, massive factories, great scientific and medical discoveries.

People saw progress on every side and believed it would go on forever.

**Spread of Democracy** Progress was also seen in government. When the American Declaration of Independence was written in 1776, all nations were ruled by titled monarchs. A century later, democracy was on the rise.

The Jewish people benefited greatly from this political change. Before 1776, there was no place on earth where Jews enjoyed the same rights as other citizens. One century later, Jews had full political equality in the United States, and in most countries of Western and Central Europe.

**But In Russia . . .** But in Russia, things were different. The Russians were slow to adopt the new scientific inventions. The Czars hated the ideals of democracy. And, although the Jewish community of Russia was the largest in the world, it was treated with dreadful cruelty.

Under one of the czars, Nicholas I, Jewish boys between the ages of eight and twelve were taken from their homes and sent to serve in the Russian army—for thirty years and more! These poor children were stationed far from home, and were often starved and beaten. Those who survived were often forced to convert to Christianity.

**Alexander II** In 1855, a new czar came to the throne—Alexander II, and with him, progress.

Alexander was interested in the inventions of the West. He cared about improving business, industry, art, and literature. He gave more freedom to the Russian people.

He helped the Jews, too. He ended the drafting of Jewish children. He allowed Jews to enroll in public high schools and universities.

**A New Haman**   The hopes for the future which Alexander II inspired were shattered in 1881 when revolutionaries set off a bomb under his coach. When he died, his son Alexander III took revenge.

He canceled most of the rights his father had granted. And he turned his special fury against the Jews, even though his father's assassins were not Jewish. Alexander III passed laws that forced our people out of their homes and schools, and made it almost impossible for them to earn a living.

Worse, he encouraged riots against the Jews. The government gave permission to the Christian population to attack, loot, and destroy Jewish communities. These official riots became known as *pogroms*, from the Russian word for "devastation."

The czar's intention was stated by a leading official: "Drive a third out, convert a third to Christianity, starve a third."

**Exodus**   Few Jews converted, but millions fled Russia. Between 1881 and 1924, more than 2.25 million people—one of every five Jews in the world—moved from Eastern Europe to the United States. This country changed from a distant outpost of Judaism to a major center. One measure of this change is that during World War I there were more Jewish soldiers in the American army than there had been Jews in the whole country during the Civil War!

Most of the Jews who left Eastern Europe came to the New World. Some went to Europe or South Africa. But there were still others whose only goal was to live in Eretz Yisrael.

**A New Vision**   There had always been Jews ready to face any danger to live in the Holy Land. Their goal, however, had been to pray and study, and thereby to speed the coming of the Messiah. They survived in poverty, owing their meager existence to charity from Jews in Europe and America.

The new immigrants had a different vision. They wanted to farm the soil of the Holy Land, and make it once again a land of

Sir Moses Montefiore, the British banker who financed new settlements in the Holy Land.

milk and honey. In most of Europe, Jews had not been allowed to own land or to be farmers, and anti-Semites charged that Jews were unable to do real work. The young Jewish pioneers—in Hebrew, *halutzim* —were determined to prove that Jews could work as well as anyone.

**Earlier Projects in the Land**   A few other people had similar ideas. A wealthy English Jew, Moses Montefiore, had spent most of his long life (he lived to be 101) and much of his fortune trying to build up the country so that the Jews of Palestine could live without charity. Among his many gifts were a girls' school and a windmill to grind flour for the Jews of Jerusalem. This windmill still stands today.

In 1870, a French organization, the *Alliance Israélite Universelle*, founded Mikveh Israel (the hope of Israel), the first Jewish agricultural school in Palestine. Though the school struggled in its early years, it survived to become the leading agricultural institution in Israel.

**BILU**   But the days of glory for Israeli agriculture were distant when the first group of Russian pioneers arrived in Palestine in 1882. Just a handful of young people, about a dozen men and one woman, came from an organization called BILU. The name was taken from the initials of words spoken by the prophet Isaiah:

By now a well-known city landmark, the Montefiore windmill stands on a beautiful hilltop in Jerusalem. Over a century ago it helped support one of the first communities to live outside the Old City.

Idealistic members of the BILU movement founded Rishon Le-Zion, one of the first Jewish farming communities of modern times. They are shown here many years after their pioneering days.

*Bet Yaakov l'chu v'naylcha*
(House of Jacob, come let us go up.)

These young halutzim were real heroes. They came from comfortable homes and had good educations. Yet they gave up all their comforts in order to rebuild the Jewish homeland.

Unfortunately, their courage and devotion were not enough. They had almost no money, and little knowledge of farming—especially of farming in the rocks and swamps of Eretz Yisrael. Some died of malaria. Others left their barren, rocky farms and moved into the towns. Others returned to Russia or left for America.

Yet for every settler who died or left, several new halutzim arrived.

**The Yishuv In Danger** A new group of pioneers began to develop late in the nineteenth century. This new Jewish community in Eretz Yisrael was known as the *Yishuv* (Hebrew for "settlement").

The Yishuv was barely surviving. The settlers were overworked, sick, and discouraged. The dream of a rebuilt Jewish homeland was in danger of collapsing.

Then, suddenly, large sums of money arrived from Europe.

Most of the halutzim had come from cities in Eastern Europe; they knew nothing about farming. But they overcame their lack of experience and built a new way of life, working and living in the fields of their new land.

Baron Edmond de Rothschild, right, contributed huge sums of money to the early Jewish settlements of Palestine. He is shown with Sir Herbert Samuel, the first High Commissioner of British Palestine.

The small colonies were saved from starvation. But who had sent the funds?

Soon it became clear that the money that kept coming to Palestine could be the gift only of an extraordinarily rich man. That man was the leading Jew of France—Baron Edmond de Rothschild.

**Baron de Rothschild**   There are different stories of how Rothschild became interested in the Yishuv. The most appealing states that a Russian rabbi came to see him. The rabbi did not know French, and spoke with such a stammer that he could communicate only by singing his tale of the Yishuv in Hebrew, and having the song translated!

The story of dedicated Jews starving in Palestine for the sake of the Jewish homeland transformed the rich man's life. During the next fifty years he bought 125,000 acres of land for Jewish settlements. His experts helped the Yishuv drain swamps, develop irrigation, and start new industries, such as perfume manufacturing and winemaking.

During his lifetime, the Baron gave more money to Palestine than all the rest of the Jews in the world combined!

**The Results**   Thanks to the determination and selflessness of the halutzim and the generosity of Baron de Rothschild, the land began to revive. By 1897, only fifteen years after the first BILU arrived, a new era in Palestine had begun. Twenty farm settlements were being worked by 5000 Jews. They were only 10 percent of all the Yishuv. Most of the rest lived in Jerusalem and other holy cities, still relying on charity.

But the first steps toward placing the Jewish homeland into Jewish hands had been taken.

## SUMMARY

Nineteenth-century progress in science, industry and government, which changed North America and much of Europe, barely touched Russia. The only czar who was interested in such ideas, Alexander II, was murdered. His son, Alexander III, launched a campaign against the Jews, especially through organized riots called *pogroms*. Millions of Jews left for America, but a handful, known as the BILU, went to Palestine. Their first efforts at farming were not successful, but, thanks in part to the generosity of Baron Edmond de Rothschild, many settlements survived. By 1897, the Yishuv—the Jewish community in Palestine—was a reality.

## Chapter Six

# One Man Changes History

**O**n a dismal winter morning in 1895, 5000 soldiers stood in a square at the Paris Military Academy. A general sat on horseback. A man in a captain's uniform was brought before him. The man was a Jew, accused of being a traitor.

"Alfred Dreyfus," said the general, "you are unworthy to bear arms. In the name of the French Republic, I take away your rank."

Soldiers ripped the buttons from the captain's uniform, and hurried him off to prison.

And all the while, Alfred Dreyfus kept crying out, "I am innocent."

**The Reporter**   These events were witnessed by a tall, handsome reporter for an Austrian newspaper. He, too, was a Jew. His name was Theodor Herzl.

Herzl could not forget that morning. He was troubled because he believed that Dreyfus was innocent of the charge of giving military secrets to the enemy. But what disturbed him most was the crowd in the streets that shouted, "Death to the Jews!" Even if it were true that Dreyfus was a traitor, was it right to call for the death of every French Jew?

Dreyfus was indeed innocent, though it took nine years to clear his name. Throughout that time, the cries of the French crowd kept ringing in the ears of Theodor Herzl. He wrote:

> The Dreyfus case . . . embodies the desire of the vast majority of the French to condemn a Jew, and to condemn all Jews in this one Jew.

**The Jewish State**   Herzl could not rest. The whole Western world believed in progress. Jews had believed that progress would mean an end of anti-Semitism. Yet Herzl could see that this was not true. No nation in Europe was more advanced than

This French newspaper (left) identified Alfred Dreyfus as a traitor. The French word is not hard to find.

An artist's drawing from the period shows Dreyfus being stripped of his military rank (below).

France, but the Dreyfus case showed that Jewish rights there were in mortal danger. If the Jews were not safe in France, where could they ever be truly free?

Then it came to him—an idea so simple that he believed it could change the world.

The Jews must have a home of their own.

There had not been an independent Jewish state since the days of the Maccabees, but that did not stop Herzl. The French had a French state. The Germans had a German state. The Jews should have a state, too.

In the heat of inspiration, he wrote a small book, *The Jewish State*. In it he prophesied:

> The Jews who will it shall have their state. We shall at last live as free men on our own soil and die peacefully in our own homeland.

**Chovevel Zion**   Herzl thought his idea was new. He later said that if he had known that others before him had had the same idea, he would never have written his book.

Fifty years earlier, rabbis in Eastern Europe had suggested resettling Eretz Yisrael. Groups had formed in Russia called *Chovevei Zion*, "The Lovers of Zion." They had helped set up Mikveh Israel, the struggling agricultural school in Palestine. They had inspired the halutzim to build farm communities.

Nonetheless, Herzl's book was electrifying. Here was a successful writer living in a free Western country outlining a plan for the rebirth of a state that had not existed for some twenty centuries. People described the book as a "bolt of lightning," a brilliant flash, giving a glimpse of a new age.

**First Zionist Congress**   Herzl saw that it was not enough to have a dream of a Jewish state. He needed an organization to make the dream come true.

His idea for building that organization was simple, but startling. He would organize a congress that would represent the Jews of the world. There had never in all of history been an official, worldwide gathering of Jews, but Herzl was convinced it could be done. Using his own money, he started a weekly newspaper to publicize his idea of a movement to create a Jewish state in Eretz Yisrael. He called the movement Zionism.

His plan became a reality. On August 29, 1897, the First Zionist Congress met in Basel, Switzerland. Some 200 leaders

Theodor Herzl, the foun-
der of modern Zionism.

from Europe, America, and North Africa voted to form a World
Zionist Organization to create "for the Jewish people a home in
Palestine secured by public law."

Herzl wrote in his diary, "Today I created the Jewish State. In
five years, perhaps, and certainly in fifty, everyone will see it."

Exactly fifty years later, in 1947, the United Nations voted to
create the State of Israel.

**Frustration and Troubles** Progress toward that dream was
painfully slow. The rulers of the world were not as eager as Herzl
to solve "the Jewish problem." Herzl traveled tirelessly, freely
spending his own money and strength, but the Turkish sultan
would not give official permission for Jewish settlement in Eretz
Yisrael. There were already settlements; but the Turks, while not
forbidding them, had never officially approved them. Herzl
feared that the Yishuv could be wiped out overnight.

Meanwhile, the situation of the Jews in Eastern Europe was
growing worse. In 1903, a terrible pogrom in the Russian town of
Kishinev shook the Jewish world. The new century had begun

with a massacre clearly organized by the Russian government. Herzl was desperate to find a home for Russian Jewry.

**The Uganda Proposal** At this moment, the British offered a proposal. They would grant permission for Jews to settle in Africa, in the colony of Uganda.

Herzl was delighted, and proposed to the Sixth Zionist Congress that the idea be studied. Though Uganda could never replace Zion in Jewish hearts, it could provide "a shelter for the night" until a permanent home in Eretz Yisrael could be created.

The Jews of Western Europe approved Herzl's proposal. How-

Delegates to the First Zionist Congress. Herzl appears in the large photo at center.

ever, the Russian Jews, the people who were supposed to benefit from the Uganda plan, stormed out of the Congress. They refused to turn their attention from the only proper goal of the Zionist movement—a Jewish state in the land of Israel, the ancient homeland of their people.

**Unity at All Costs**   Herzl was stunned. "These people have a rope around their necks," he said, "and still they refuse."

But he had always insisted that the Zionist movement remain united. He called a special conference, and there agreed to abandon the Uganda plan. The Jewish state could be only in Eretz Yisrael.

**End and Beginning**   Unity had been restored, but it had taken the last bit of Herzl's strength. He had not been well for some time. Now his health was shattered. He took a vacation, but even then he could not stop working. Greatly weakened, he died of pneumonia on July 3, 1904.

The man whom many considered a modern prophet, was gone at the age of forty-four.

The grave of Theodor Herzl, in Jerusalem. Can you read the Hebrew word inscribed on the stone?

Just nine years had passed since that dismal winter morning when Herzl had heard the French masses call for the death of the Jews. In that tiny space of time he had transformed a people. Now the Jews were organized, calling for a state of their own.

Theodor Herzl is known as the Father of Political Zionism.

**The Monument**   Herzl was taken to his grave by a huge throng of weeping Jews. He was buried in Vienna; but he knew that would not be his final resting place. With total faith in the Zionist cause, he left instructions that he be reburied in the Jewish state.

The Jewish people did not forget. In 1949, the citizens of the new State of Israel brought his coffin from Vienna and buried it on a hill overlooking Jerusalem. His tomb is marked with a simple black stone. On it is engraved one word: Herzl.

### SUMMARY

Theodor Herzl was shocked by the unjust treatment of a French Jewish soldier, Captain Alfred Dreyfus, and decided that Jews could be safe only if they had a state of their own. His book, *The Jewish State*, attracted world attention. Herzl then organized the First Zionist Congress, the first official gathering of world Jewish leaders. Through the Congress and the World Zionist Organization, Herzl changed the spirit of the Jewish people, and established the organizations which would create the State of Israel.

## Chapter Seven

# To Build a Land

**O**n a hot, damp September morning in 1906, an old steamship pulled into the harbor of Jaffa. The young Jews on board had left Russia to settle in Eretz Yisrael. Now they strained to catch glimpses of the port city from which the prophet Jonah is said to have begun his famous journey over 2600 years ago.

Jaffa was supposed to be the gateway to their dreams. But once the immigrants were on land, the dreams turned into nightmares. The streets were filthy, the buildings decayed, the port filled with beggars.

**One Who Stayed** For many Jews, such sights were the beginning of the end. This depressing greeting, followed by back-breaking farm work, poverty, hunger, and malaria, drove them back to Western lands. Perhaps as many as nine of every ten immigrants later left the country.

But the ship that arrived in 1906 carried one among that band of a few hundred who became the real builders of the State of Israel. He was a short, stocky, twenty-year-old who would not be turned aside from his vision of a Jewish homeland. His first sight of Jaffa merely drove him to walk all afternoon and into the night until he reached the orange groves of Petah Tikva. The next morning he was carting fertilizer to the orange groves.

Such was the introduction to Eretz Yisrael of the man who would be the first Prime Minister of the State of Israel—David Ben-Gurion.

**The Second Aliyah** Ben Gurion was part of the wave of immigration known as the "Second Aliyah."

*Aliyah* is a Hebrew word that means "going up." In the days of the Temple, it meant "going up on pilgrimage to Jerusalem." In the synagogue, it means "going up to the *bimah*" to read from the

Torah. In modern times, it has also come to mean "going up to the land of Israel"—immigration.

There have been several waves of immigration to Palestine. The First Aliyah began with the BILU settlers in 1882 and continued until 1903.

The Second Aliyah began in 1904, when pogroms in Russia sent Jews fleeing in all directions. It was also the year of the death of Herzl, which moved some to make an extra effort to preserve his dream of a Jewish state.

**Ideals of the Second Aliyah**  The members of the Second Aliyah recognized that the key to building a Jewish homeland was the creation of a Jewish labor force.

Before 1904, most of the workers in the Jewish settlements were not Jewish. The Jewish settlements used six times as many Arab workers as Jewish workers. The Arabs had certain skills in

A young David Ben Gurion stands in the center of a group of agricultural workers. The immigrants of the Second Aliyah brought energy, enthusiasm, and determination to the Zionist movement.

The pioneers had no tractors, just old-fashioned tools and field animals. Plowing the land meant long days of strenuous labor.

farming and construction, and they would work for very low wages.

The halutzim of the Second Aliyah saw that this placed the Jewish community at the whim of Arab workers. Worse, it separated the Jews from their own land. The halutzim were determined to rebuild both the land and its people, to turn the Jews of Palestine into a nation of workers. As they labored, they sang:

*Anu banu artzah livnot u-l'hibanot ba*
We have come to the land to build and to be rebuilt in it.

**A Difficult Task**   The major rebuilding the halutzim had to do was the land itself. The hills were worn down to bare rock. The valleys were clogged with the washed-out soil and the streams had become marshes. These had turned into malarial swamps. A bite from the mosquito which carries the malaria germs could mean fever and death. Yet the Jews had nowhere else to go, since this was the only land in Palestine for sale.

The halutzim drained the swamps. Almost all of them contracted malaria. Many died, but the rest carried on.

They built roads to replace bare donkey tracks, so that they could move wagons and trucks. They planted trees by the millions to stop the erosion of mountain slopes.

Little time was left for rest or recreation or material things. As Rachel Ben-Zvi, wife of the future second President of Israel, wrote: "Our household does not require too much bother. In a minute the straw mat is aired, the tin cups are rinsed, everything is done and we are free [to work the land]."

**Working Together**  The best-known result of the Second Aliyah ideal is the collective farm, in which everyone shares equally in governing the community, in doing the work and in enjoying its benefits.

The idea came about almost by accident.

In 1909, a privately-owned farm near the Sea of Galilee was failing. Its Jewish workers requested a voice in running it.

An experiment was tried. Seven excellent farmhands were given seventy-five acres to plant. They did all their planning together, and shared all the work.

At the end of a year, they had made a substantial profit!

In 1911, another small group decided to carry on the experiment. They created a settlement at the southern end of the Sea of Galilee, where the Jordan River begins its journey to the Dead Sea. They named the settlement *Degania* ("God's Grain"). It, too, was a success.

**Kvutza and Kibbutz and Moshav**  A farm in which everyone shares in the planning and the profits is known as a *kvutza*. More and more of these farms were opened, and Degania became known as the "mother of k'vutzot."

The kvutza was very small. Eventually, a larger settlement was attempted. Many predicted that fair sharing on a bigger scale was impossible. However, the larger collective settlement was successful also. Such a place is called a *kibbutz*.

In a third type of settlement, individual farmers lease their own land, but join together to buy and share heavy machinery and supplies, and to sell their produce. This type of settlement is called a *moshav*.

Today, there are some 750 of these three types of settlements, and one-tenth of the Jewish population of Israel lives in them.

**Defense**   Having a settlement meant being willing to defend it from attack.

This idea seems obvious, but it was quite startling in 1907. There had been no Jewish armed force in 1800 years. Even though the Jewish settlements were easy targets for thieves, defense was left to hired non-Jews.

Ten Jewish men decided to change this. They themselves would do guard duty. But how could these volunteers prove their ability to Jewish farm managers? In one case, the young men stole a mule from under the nose of an Arab guard. They returned it the next morning to the manager. The animal's loss had not yet been detected.

The Jewish guards were hired.

**Ha-Shomer**   In 1909, Jewish workers organized their defense forces under the leadership of Israel Shohat, a young Russian of the Second Aliyah. The organization was called *Ha-Shomer* — "The Watchman."

Members of Ha-Shomer were like a posse of cowboys, galloping on horseback to defend their fellow Jews. They looked more like an Arab legion than a Jewish group, for they often wore Arab clothes as a sign of friendship to Muslims who wished to live in peace. But Arabs who attacked were met with force.

Ha-Shomer chose to remain small. Its original unit numbered eight. Two years later it had grown only to twenty-six. (One of those rejected for membership was David Ben-Gurion.) Yet this tiny band successfully defended the lonely Jewish outposts, and created the basis for what would be the most efficient army in the world.

**Language for a Nation**   The Second Aliyah was also determined to make Hebrew the language of the land.

Today this seems like a natural choice, but not at that time. The native language of most of the immigrants was Russian, Polish, or Yiddish. Moreover, Hebrew was the holy tongue of our people, and Orthodox Jews strongly objected to hearing the language of the Torah used to say, "Go clean the cattle barn."

There was another problem. Hebrew was an ancient language that had no words for many aspects of modern life. It had no vocabulary for "radio," "telephone," "babysitter," or "silverware."

This problem was met by a very unusual kind of hero, a small Russian scholar who took the Hebrew name Eliezer Ben-Yehuda.

A band of Ha-Shomer, the first Jewish defense force of modern times.

**Eliezer Ben-Yehuda**  Ben-Yehuda came to Palestine in 1881, even before the BILU settlers. He wasn't part of a wave of immigration. He was a lone man possessed with an idea. He believed that Hebrew was the only language capable of uniting the Jewish people in a Jewish homeland.

At the age of twenty-three, he and his bride set sail for Palestine. They vowed never again to speak any language but Hebrew. They had to make terrible sacrifices to keep this pledge. Orthodox Jews, who thought everyday use of Hebrew was sacrilege, would not speak to them. At times they nearly starved. Often no one would play with their children. When Ben-Yehuda's wife died, she was refused burial in a Jewish cemetery.

Despite all, the Ben-Yehuda family spoke only Hebrew. And Eliezer Ben-Yehuda compiled a brilliant dictionary which in-

Eliezer Ben-Yehuda (above), a
different kind of hero.

Today, people come from all
over the world to study Hebrew in Israel. In this class-
room (right) a Christian nun
and several Jewish immi-
grants are learning the language of the Bible.

cluded new words he had created to make Hebrew usable in all areas of modern life.

**Victory for Hebrew**  Ben-Yehuda triumphed. Schools began to teach Hebrew. The halutzim of the Second Aliyah became his allies, and struggled to learn the Hebrew language even as they struggled to conquer the land. At times they were almost fanatic. When a girl was stricken with malaria and began to rave in Russian, her nurse criticized her for not using Hebrew!

The key battle for Hebrew took place in 1913. A German-Jewish group founded a technological school in Haifa, whose official language was to be German. Students and teachers went on strike. The school could not open until it was agreed that its language would be Hebrew.

In later years, Israel was to be flooded with immigrants who spoke dozens of languages. The Jewish State found, as Ben-Yehuda had foreseen, that the Hebrew language was an important force that helped make them one people.

**Today ...**  Today Israel is a modern state with thriving farms, fine schools, handsome cities, tall forests, and millions of proud inhabitants. It is hard for us to imagine that in our grandparents' time it was a poor and dangerous place. It was rebuilt by a tiny number of brave men and women.

All of them sacrificed comfort and safety for the sake of the Jewish homeland. Many lost their lives.

Because they were loyal and brave and unselfish, many lived to see, and to become the leaders of, the reborn State of Israel.

### SUMMARY

David Ben-Gurion was one of the immigrants who came to Palestine in the second great wave of Jewish immigration—the Second Aliyah. The goal of the Second Aliyah was to rebuild both the land and the Jewish people. Jewish farms began to use Jewish workers and Jewish guards. The first Jewish armed force in modern times, *Ha-Shomer*, was created. Collective farms—the *kvutza*, the *kibbutz*, and the *moshav*—were developed. Thanks in part to the pioneering work of Eliezer Ben-Yehuda, Hebrew became the language of the Jewish state. The key pioneers—the *halutzim*—were few in number, but their dedication was total. They were in large part responsible for Israel as we know it today.

Tel Aviv is one of the youngest and fastest growing cities in the world. In this famous picture (above left) the city's first settlers gather to divide the sand dunes into lots for streets and houses. The year was 1909. The next photo (below left) shows Tel Aviv only twelve years later. Today, Tel Aviv is a large, modern, and bustling city (above).

## SPECIAL TOPIC

### Children of the Kibbutz

"Working together." That is the theme of people on a kibbutz. This includes the raising of children. At most kibbutzim, children are raised together. Instead of living with their parents, they live in a children's house. There the community provides grownups to take care of them. It provides places to sleep and places to eat, places to study and places to play.

Children see their own parents regularly, during the day or after work. They have fun together before the children go back to their house, and the parents to theirs. This sounds strange to us, but the children seem to grow up every bit as happy as children who come from "normal" homes.

On this kibbutz children live in their own houses, separate from their parents. In the baby house (left), kibbutz workers feed the community's youngest members. The woman in the second picture (right) has found an easy way to move a group of toddlers around the kibbutz.

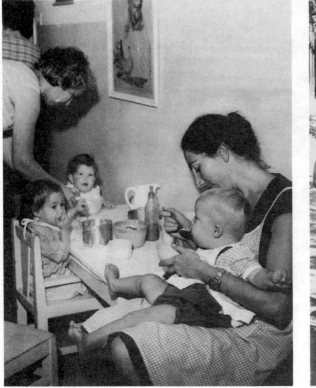 

## Chapter Eight

# The First World War

In June 1914, an Austrian prince was assassinated. This incident was turned into a cause for war. What everyone expected to be a short series of battles lasted four years. This was the First World War.

The great nations fought for power and prestige; and they chose whatever allies seemed necessary. Britain and France joined forces with Russia. This meant that the two most powerful democracies of Europe were allied to Czar Nicholas, the worst tyrant and anti-Semite in the world.

On the opposing side were the so-called "Central Powers"—Germany, Austria, and Turkey. Two of the developing leaders of Europe were linked to the rulers of a decaying Asian empire.

**Fate of the Yishuv** Regardless of who was winning, the fighting in Europe hurt the Jews of Palestine. The Yishuv depended on food and financial help from abroad. Most of these supplies were choked off by the war. Thousands of our people starved to death.

Many were able to fight, however, and they were willing to support their Turkish rulers. The Turks were fighting the Czar, the man most hated by the Jews.

But the Turkish Sultan was afraid. Most of the halutzim had been born in Russia: if given weapons, wouldn't they fight for the Russian cause? Jews who offered to organize a militia were sent into exile, "never to return." These included David Ben-Gurion and his close friend, Yitzhak Ben-Zvi (who would become the second president of Israel).

**Fighting the Turks** The cruelty of the Turks forced the Jews to fight against the Turkish Empire. Leading the fight were two of the most interesting and colorful men in Zionist history: Vladimir Jabotinsky and Josef Trumpeldor.

Jabotinsky and Trumpeldor had much in common. They were both born in Russia in the year 1880. Both had tried to be loyal Russians. Jabotinsky was a brilliant writer—at the age of seventeen he translated the works of Edgar Allen Poe into Russian. Trumpeldor, trained as a dentist, fought in the Russian army against the Japanese. Though his left arm was shattered and had to be amputated, he insisted on staying at the front. His superiors awarded him a medal for bravery, and made him an officer—the first Jewish officer in the history of the Russian army.

Yet as the pogroms against the Jews continued, both men saw that the Russians would never accept Jews as equals. Trumpeldor settled in Palestine, only to be exiled by the Turks to Egypt. There he met Jabotinsky, who had been traveling as a newspaperman and spokesman for Zionism. The two resolved to create a legion of Jewish soldiers to battle the Turks.

**The Zion Mule Corps**  They hoped to send Jewish soldiers into Palestine. The British would accept Jewish support, but only for the fighting in Turkey—and only as mule-drivers transporting ammunition.

Vladimir Jabotinsky, a gifted writer and speaker, convinced the British to establish the Jewish Legion.

Josef Trumpeldor, an experienced soldier and hero of the Yishuv.

Disappointed, Jabotinsky dropped out of the project. Trumpeldor's view was that, as long as the enemy was the Sultan, any battle "leads to Zion."

In 1915, some 500 Jews from Palestine and Egypt were accepted into the "Zion Mule Corps." Their duty was to bring supplies to the lines, often under heavy fire. Seven members of the Corps died in action. Many more were wounded—including Trumpeldor.

The heroes of the Zion Mule Corps were the first Jews ever to serve as a unit within the army of a modern state. The reputation of these men, who risked their lives while wearing the Star of David on their shoulders, spread throughout the Zionist world.

**In England** While the Yishuv was struggling for survival, and the Zion Mule Corps was under fire in Turkey, a very different battle for Zionism was being fought in England. The Russian-born Jew who led this battle was then the world's leading Zionist. One day he would be the first President of the State of Israel.

His name was Chaim Weizmann.

Weizmann grew up in a family that dreamed of a rebuilt Zion even before the Zionist movement existed. He organized support

Chaim Weizmann, scientist and statesman, international spokesman for the Zionist cause.

for the movement, and attended all but the first of the World Zionist Congresses. He soon became a World Zionist leader. He was not yet thirty when he led the opposition to Herzl's plan for a temporary homeland in Uganda.

His work as a research chemist had brought him to England, where he met a leading British statesman, Lord Arthur James Balfour. Balfour tried to convince Weizmann that the Jews should accept Britain's offer of a homeland in Uganda.

It was Weizmann who convinced Balfour that Palestine was

the only place that could mobilize the loyalty, energy, and commitment of the Jewish people. Balfour became an enthusiastic Zionist.

**Weizmann in Wartime** During World War I, the British had a problem which only a chemist could solve. The country needed a steady supply of the chemical acetone to make ammunition. Before the war, this chemical had come from Germany. Where would the acetone come from to fight Germany?

Weizmann was able to provide the answer. He succeeded in producing acetone from corn, which was plentiful in England.

Through his political and chemical work, Weizmann came to know most of the political figures in England. The time would come when these contacts would help the Zionist cause.

**Protect the Canal!** The Turks launched two attacks on the Suez Canal. They were beaten back both times, but the British saw that the situation was dangerous. The canal was the key link between Britain and India. It connected the Mediterranean to the Red Sea, which cut the shipping distance from England to India by more than 4000 miles.

The British realized that the Arabs could not be relied on to defend the Canal. An excellent defense, however, would be a strong Jewish settlement in Palestine.

**The Balfour Declaration** Weizmann and his colleagues encouraged such thinking. It appeared that the British government was ready to announce its support for the creation of a Jewish homeland.

A small but influential group of wealthy English Jews fought this move. They were afraid Zionism might damage their position in England. In England, they had enjoyed full political rights for only one generation. Now Zionists were showing loyalty to Palestine.

It was a strange moment. A modern Christian country was ready to support the Jewish dream of returning to Zion. And a group of wealthy Jews was standing in the way.

At last, the President of the United States, Woodrow Wilson, cabled the British government his approval of a Jewish homeland. This broke the deadlock. On November 2, 1917, Lord Balfour, by then Foreign Secretary of Great Britain, issued a letter which stated:

His Majesty's Government view with favour the establishment in Palestine of a national home for the Jewish people.

France, Italy, and the United States officially agreed.

**Worldwide Reaction**  The Zionists had won approval of a truly amazing statement. The Yishuv was only thirty-five years old. No one knew what a "national home" was. There was no definition of the "Jewish people." Yet the most powerful nation in the world had announced its approval of a Jewish home in Palestine.

The Jews of Britain and Russia were overjoyed. The Jews of the United States celebrated with large parades.

But in Palestine, the Balfour Declaration filled the starving Yishuv with terror. Would the Declaration convince the Turks that Jews were loyal to Britain? How long would it be before the fear of Jewish disloyalty became the excuse for a massacre?

**Liberating Palestine**  At this dramatic moment, Vladimir Jabotinsky rose to his role in history: he at last persuaded the British to accept a Jewish legion for combat in Palestine. The first volunteers were veterans of the Zion Mule Corps. Jabotinsky looked for more volunteers in England and the United States. From America came Ben-Gurion and Ben-Zvi, both eager to end their exile.

While the Jewish Legion was being formed, the British launched their attack in Palestine under the command of General Edmund Allenby. Within a few weeks, Allenby drove the Turks from Jaffa. On December 11, 1917, he marched into the City of David to proclaim "a new era of brotherhood and peace in the Holy Land."

Allenby's arrival in Jerusalem took place on Hanukkah. On the same day, Jews celebrated both the liberation of Jerusalem from the Turks in 1917—and from the Syrian Greeks more than 2000 years before.

Winter rains prevented Allenby from completing his conquest. That winter was the worst for the Yishuv. The Turks attacked the Jewish farm settlements, mercilessly robbing and murdering.

At last spring came, and Allenby—now joined by the Jewish Legion—marched north. The Turks fled. Jabotinsky himself led a Jewish unit across the Jordan River in pursuit. By September

After participating in the British conquest of Jerusalem in 1917, these Jewish Legion soldiers posed at the Western Wall.

1918, the last of the Turkish forces in Palestine had been defeated. Two months later, World War I ended.

**Results of World War I**   The war had brought terrible misery. In 1914, the Jewish population in Eretz Yisrael was 85,000. At the end of the war, it was fewer than 55,000. Nearly one-third had died of starvation, illness, or exposure.

But what the Jews had achieved! They had proved that they could participate as equals in anything that a great power could undertake, even in the longest and bloodiest war the world had yet known. And Great Britain, with the support of the United States, had declared that the Jews were entitled to a national home in Palestine.

**An Arab Welcome**   The Jews had also made common cause with another group long oppressed by the Turks — the Arabs. During the war, Chaim Weizmann had met with the Emir Feisal, one of the most important of the Arab leaders. The two men had agreed that there was room enough in Palestine to fulfill the dreams of both Arabs and Jews. As Feisal was to write:

Chaim Weizmann, left, with the Arab leader Emir Feisal in 1918.

We Arabs . . . look with the deepest sympathy on the Zionist movement. . . . We will wish the Jews a most hearty welcome home.

## SUMMARY

During World War I, the Turks were cruel to the Yishuv. This forced the Jews to fight with Great Britain against the Turks. The first Jewish unit to join the British was the Zion Mule Corps, organized by Joseph Trumpeldor. Vladimir Jabotinsky organized the Jewish Legion, which fought with General Allenby to drive the Turks from Palestine. Chaim Weizmann succeeded in obtaining from the British government the Balfour Declaration, which gave offical support to the concept of a Jewish national home in Palestine. Arab support for the idea seemed to promise a future of peace.

# The Road to Independence

## Chapter Nine

# From Cooperation to Conflict

**O**ne morning in 1920, Josef Trumpeldor was eating breakfast at a settlement in northern Palestine. Then word came that another settlement, Tel Hai, was being attacked by Arabs.

Trumpeldor grabbed his gun. Dodging Arab bullets, the one-armed soldier and a group of followers managed to reach the Tel Hai settlers. Suddenly Trumpeldor realized that, in the rush, someone had left the gate open. He dashed out to close it.

Shots rang out. Trumpeldor fell.

The Arabs were forced to retreat, but it was too late to save the Jewish hero. Though he died, his life became an inspiration. His last words were never forgotten:

"It is good to die for our country."

**Causes of Anger** What had happened to Emir Feisal's promise of a "hearty welcome home" to the Jews? How had the welcome turned to bloodshed?

In part, Feisal had exaggerated the good feelings of Arabs toward Jews. He had to admit that the Arabs who approved of Zionism were "especially the educated among us." But by 1920, even the educated Arabs had given up hoping for peace. They felt betrayed by England, France, and the Jews.

**Conflicting Promises** Britain's Balfour Declaration had promised the Jews a national home in Palestine. Some of the men involved in making this promise, including Balfour himself, sincerely believed in the Zionist cause.

But there had been another reason for issuing the Declaration. Britain was at war. The Declaration gained Jewish support for the British cause.

Britain also wanted Arab support, because the Arabs made up more than half the population of the Ottoman Empire. So the

British offered independence to Arabs who would help battle the Turks. To some, independence included Arab control of Palestine.

Despite these promises, the British secretly agreed with the French to divide control of the Middle East. England took Palestine and Iraq, while the French took Syria and Lebanon.

The Arabs were justly furious. Agreements with Weizmann were forgotten. The Arabs now demanded total control of the Middle East.

**What Might Have Been**   The League of Nations refused to "give" Palestine to Great Britain. Instead, Britain was given the duty to develop Palestine as a Jewish homeland. This responsibility was called "the British Mandate."

If Britain had fulfilled its duties under the Mandate, and if the Arabs had been given independence where they had traditionally ruled, the Middle East might have known peace.

Instead, Britain and France made a tragic mistake. They decided to keep control of the whole Middle East, except for Palestine—which they would give, as a gift, to the Arabs.

**Britain Aids the Arabs**   Even before the terms of the Mandate were final, British Colonial Secretary Winston Churchill split off all of Palestine east of the Jordan River and gave it to the Arabs. This was three-quarters of the land that was to have been the Jewish homeland! This new Arab country was known as Transjordan until 1949, and then became the Kingdom of Jordan.

Today we hear Arabs complain that Palestinian Arabs have no state of their own. Actually, the Palestinian Arabs have Jordan, a state far larger than the Jewish state of Israel.

The first British High Commissioner for Palestine was Sir Herbert Samuel, an English Jew. He established law and order. The years under his government were fairly peaceful.

Even so, Sir Herbert was under orders to make peace with the Arabs and to do as little as possible toward creating the promised Jewish national home.

**Arab Riots**   Sir Herbert left Palestine in 1925, and British favoritism toward the Arabs became more open. By 1929, the Arabs decided it was time to show their power.

The Arab leaders called on their followers to attack the Jews.

In 1938, after a week of anti-Jewish rioting, British soldiers finally stepped in to restore order. Here the British lead arrested Arabs through Jerusalem's Damascus Gate.

The frenzied masses went wild. They did not attack the armed Jews of the kibbutzim. They attacked the old, unarmed, pious worshippers in the cities. One hundred thirty-three Jews were massacred. Several hundred were wounded. Jewish property was destroyed.

The British did nothing to punish the rioters, or to prevent more riots. Naturally, the Arabs became even bolder.

Years of violence reached a climax in 1936. The Arabs launched a full-scale riot. Murder and destruction were widespread. A symbol of the Arab success was the holy city of Hebron. The Jews there were killed or driven out. Once King David's capital, Hebron held the tombs of the Patriarchs—the fathers and mothers of the Jewish people—Abraham, Isaac and Jacob, Sarah, Rebecca and Leah. Now, for the first time in thousands of years, there were no Jews in Hebron.

**Jewish Response: Self-Defense**   In the early years of the Yishuv, the cowboy-like guards of Ha-Shomer had done a brilliant job of protecting Jewish settlers. By 1920, however, a larger organization was needed for protection. It was formed with the name *Haganah*—"Defense."

Haganah was an unofficial army with two enemies—the Arabs and the British. The Arabs wanted to destroy the Jewish population. The British wanted to destroy the Haganah.

Despite pressure from both groups, Haganah showed remarkable patience. Its official policy was *havlagah*, "self-restraint." Many felt that every time a Jew was murdered, Haganah should murder some Arabs. Haganah rejected the policy of retaliation.

There were two reasons for this restraint. First, it is wrong to murder innocent people. Second, Haganah did not wish to give the British any further excuse to limit Jewish immigration.

**Jewish Response: Immigration**   More and more Jews were coming to Palestine. Some were drawn by the reports of the Zionists' accomplishments. Many more were driven by conditions in Europe, such as the 67,000 who fled from terrible persecution in Poland.

Jewish residents of Palestine developed some unusual methods of self-defense. To prevent Arabs from tossing grenades into crowded buses, they attached protective screens to the windows.

As the Nazi threat grew, the Zionists organized an immigration program, "Youth Aliyah," to bring Jewish children out of Germany. This train left Berlin in 1935, filled with children on their way to Palestine.

Then Adolf Hitler came to power in Germany, declaring he would make the country "clean of Jews." The need for a haven in Eretz Yisrael became desperate. Between 1929 and 1939, 250,000 Jewish refugees—a quarter of a million people—came to Palestine.

Many of these refugees settled in the growing cities. Others worked the land. Swamps were drained, and barren soil turned into fertile farms.

**Jewish Response: Settlements**  Building settlements for new halutzim was no simple matter. If the settlers were to spend weeks, or even days, at construction, they would be easy targets for Arab attack.

The solution was to build each new settlement in one day!

The technique for doing this was called "stockade and tower" (*Homah u-Migdal*). The night before a settlement was to be built, all the materials for it were collected and prepared at a nearby village. At daybreak, all the equipment and structures were moved to the site. By sunup, the watchtower would be standing. By noon, the outer defense wall would be in place. At twilight, a small farm was functioning—complete with cows and chickens.

Throughout the difficult years of the 1930's, Jews continued to build new settlements.

Kibbutz Hanita, a "stockade and tower" settlement, founded in 1938. It was built in only one day.

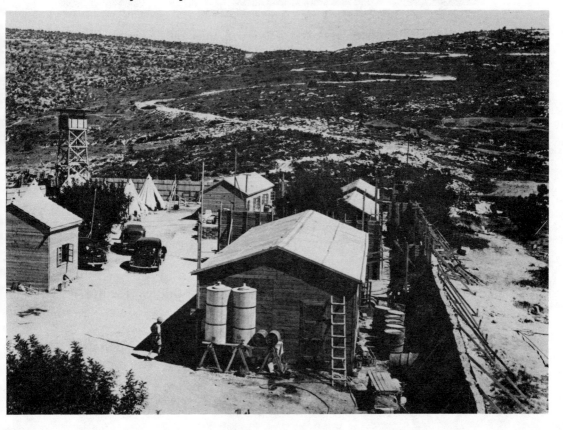

Henrietta Szold, the founder of Hadassah, and the first director of Youth Aliyah.

**Jewish Response: Health**  The land was being restored to health. So were the Jewish people. Palestine under the Turks had been a miserable place. Malaria and tuberculosis were only two of its deadly diseases. Just before World War I, an American woman named Henrietta Szold visited the country. She was horrified by the poor health conditions.

When she returned to America, she organized the women's organization known as Hadassah to improve health in Palestine. Hadassah sent physicians and nurses to set up clinics and hospitals. Hadassah established schools for physicians, dentists, and nurses. It taught mothers how to take care of their children.

Within a few decades, Hadassah raised the health standards of Eretz Yisrael from among the worst to the finest in the whole Middle East.

**The British White Paper**  The Jews were building for life— land, farms, health. The Arabs were working to destroy— murder, looting, riots.

The world situation was growing worse. Adolf Hitler was rising in power. Arab violence in Palestine was increasing.

The British picked the worst possible response to Arab violence: they gave the Arabs everything they wanted.

In 1939, Great Britain issued a document called the "White Paper." It stated that England intended to set up an independent state in Palestine with a permanent Arab majority. Jewish immigration would be cut back to 15,000 people per year for five years. Then Jewish immigration would be entirely shut off.

**Zionist Reaction**  Zionists throughout the world were appalled. If the White Paper went into effect, there would never be a Jewish homeland.

But before the Yishuv could organize against the White Paper, World War II broke out. Germany rapidly conquered most of Europe. Soon the only European nation standing against Hitler was Great Britain. All Jews had to support the battle against the

A participant in a Hadassah program, this donkey brought fresh milk to children in all parts of Jerusalem. Today the Hadassah organization continues to support quality health care in Israel, giving its name and financial backing to one of the country's finest hospitals.

In 1939, Jewish scouts took to the streets of Jerusalem to protest the White Paper.

Nazi murderers. Yet world Jewry could not accept British opposition to a Jewish settlement in Palestine.

The attitude of the Jews of Palestine was stated by David Ben-Gurion: "We shall fight the war as if there were no White Paper, and we shall fight the White Paper as if there were no war."

## SUMMARY

The Arab hopes for the future were betrayed by the French and British. The Arab leaders decided to take control of the Middle East through violence. The British did nothing to stop this violence, and thus encouraged it. The Zionists rebuilt the land, defended themselves, built new settlements, encouraged immigration, and dramatically raised the health standards of the country. The final British response was the White Paper of 1939, which announced the plan to shut off Jewish immigration and create an Arab state in Palestine.

# Chapter Ten

# The Second World War

Adolf Hitler launched World War II on September 1, 1939. In only ten months he conquered all of Europe.

Then he invaded North Africa. His goal was to cut off the supply lines of Great Britain by capturing the Suez Canal. From Suez it would be a short leap to Palestine, where he could exterminate the Jews—just as he was murdering them in Europe.

From Palestine, he also could easily swallow up the oil fields of the Middle East.

**Arabs Back Hitler**  The Arabs were eager for a Nazi victory. Some of the Arab leaders gave only quiet support to the German cause. Others worked actively for Hitler. One spent the war in Berlin, broadcasting to the Arab people the order to "rise up against Britain and her allies."

The British arrested those who were pro-Nazi when they could. One of those sent to prison was Anwar Sadat, a man destined to become a key figure in the history of the Middle East.

**England and the Yishuv**  Nazis were also setting up bases in Syria. The British wanted these bases destroyed, but could not spare soldiers for the task. They turned to the Yishuv for a solution.

A special Jewish strike force was created by the Haganah. The new group was called the Palmach. It was a very efficient commando unit, and soon the enemy bases in Syria were in ruins.

**The Tide of War Turns**  Still the Germans in North Africa marched east, closer and closer to the vital Suez Canal. The British took their stand at El Alamein, just 70 miles west of Alexandria, Egypt, and only 200 miles from the Suez Canal.

The British army, joined by many Jews of the Yishuv, held its

A Palmach unit plans for action.

ground. The Nazi advance was at last turned back. The tide of war began to turn in favor of the Allies. The Suez Canal—and the Yishuv—were safe.

**Britain and the Arabs**  Now that Britain no longer needed the help of the Jews of Palestine, it promptly extended a hand of friendship to the Arabs. The pro-Nazi Arabs were treated as allies. The Jews who had helped defend the Suez Canal were treated as enemies.

Though the British needed soldiers, they said they would accept volunteers from Palestine only if Jews and Arabs enlisted in equal numbers. Very few Arabs were interested in fighting the Nazis, while thousands of Palestinian Jews were eager to help destroy Hitler. By insisting on being "even-handed," the British kept many Jews from fighting to save their fellow Jews in Europe.

It was September 1944 before an official Jewish army unit was permitted. The Jewish Brigade fought valiantly, was one of the first units to make contact with survivors of the Nazi death camps, and played an important role in rescuing and caring for Jewish survivors.

**Moshe Dayan**  Britain's constantly shifting attitudes had a deep effect on a man who one day became one of Israel's great military leaders. The man was Moshe Dayan.

Moshe was the first child born in Palestine's first communal settlement, Degania. From his early years he took part in the Yishuv's defense, and joined the Haganah.

When World War II erupted, the British were afraid that the Haganah would fight the Arabs while the British were fighting Germany. Dayan and forty-two other Haganah officers were arrested and sentenced to ten years in prison.

Moshe Dayan, a founder of the Palmach, later one of Israel's great leaders.

But when the British found they needed a Jewish task force to attack Syria, the Haganah men were released, and Dayan became a founding member of Palmach.

He showed exceptional bravery. In one battle, he captured twelve enemy soldiers. In a later exchange of gunfire, he lost his left eye. For the rest of his life he wore a black eye patch, making him one of the most recognizable public figures.

When Britain's war effort improved, and it no longer needed Jewish help, it took back the weapons it had given the Palmach. But the Palmach, determined to be prepared for Arab attacks, broke into a British arsenal and stole back the weapons!

The British retaliated by outlawing the Palmach and the Haganah. Dayan and the Jewish defense force continued their operations, but now trained and organized in secret.

In direct defiance of the British authorities, the Haganah continued to smuggle refugees into Palestine. This 1939 Haganah poster shows the names and faces of forty-three Jewish fighters who had been captured and sent to British jails.

**Illegal Immigration**   The Haganah had no choice but to stay active. It had to bring Jews from Europe to Palestine.

The British White Paper of 1939 had announced that Jewish immigration to Palestine would be cut to 15,000 a year. Amazingly, the British maintained this policy even when it became known that the Nazis were exterminating more than 15,000 Jews every few days.

The Haganah undertook to rescue Jews by smuggling them from Europe into Palestine. By the time the State of Israel was created in 1948, more than 100,000 Jews had been saved from death "illegally."

**Doors Closed Everywhere**   The world was closed to the Jews. They could not survive in Europe. A few entered Palestine—legally and illegally. A handful was admitted to America. Some found refuge in isolated places like Hong Kong and Shanghai, China.

For six million, there was no escape.

The horror of this tragic period is illustrated by the story of two ships, filled with refugees.

One crossed the Atlantic just before the war. It was refused by the United States, Canada, and all of Latin America. After searching desperately for a port in the United States, it had to return to Hamburg, Germany. There its passengers were murdered by the Nazis.

The second refugee ship, the *Struma,* a rickety old vessel, escaped from Rumania in 1941, and headed east. The British would not permit it to land in Palestine. It was kept in a Turkish harbor for two terrible months of hunger and panic. At last the unseaworthy vessel was towed out to sea—where it sank. More than 700 men, women, and children drowned because no one would give these Jews a corner of land on which to live.

**"Blessed Is the Match"**   The war dragged on for four years. The Yishuv tried desperately to aid the Jews of Europe. One attempt created a heroine of modern Israel.

Her name was Hanna Senesch.

Hanna had left her family in Hungary at the age of eighteen, and settled in Palestine. Only a few months after her arrival, World War II broke out, and she wondered if there might be some way for her to return to Europe to rescue her mother and other stranded Jews.

Hanna Senesch parachuted into Nazi-held territory and gave her life in an attempt to rescue Hungarian Jews. Her courage lives on through her poetry.

She joined a daring group of thirty-two young Jews who parachuted into Nazi-occupied Europe. Several had ingenious exploits to steal Hungarian uniforms. When Hungarian mobs would round up Jews, the disguised group—pretending to be Hungarian soldiers—took charge of the arrested people and smuggled them to safety.

Hanna was less fortunate. She was betrayed and arrested by the Nazis. Her life was ended by a firing squad when she was only twenty-three.

The bravery Hanna Senesch showed to her judges and executioners became an inspiration to the Jews who were fighting to build a Jewish state. She expressed that bravery in a poem, *Blessed Is the Match,* which became known and loved throughout Israel:

Blessed is the match that is consumed in kindling flame.
Blessed is the flame that burns in the secret fastness of the heart.
Blessed is the heart with strength to stop its beating for honor's sake.
Blessed is the match that is consumed in kindling flame.

**Only One War Ends**   World War II ended in 1945. Hitler was dead. But there was little rejoicing in Palestine. The Nazis had succeeded in butchering six million Jews.

In addition, the Yishuv still had its own war to face. Despite everything that had happened to the Jewish people, the British still held fast to their White Paper of 1939: There would be no Jewish state.

The Yishuv renewed its fight for its homeland.

### SUMMARY

The Yishuv was eager to fight against Hitler. The British used Jewish soldiers when the need for help was desperate, but otherwise tried to keep the Jews unarmed. Moshe Dayan's life was deeply affected by this constant change of policy. The Haganah continued to rescue Jews from Europe and to bring them to Palestine illegally. The Jewish Brigade and Hanna Senesch were Jews who fought bravely in Europe. After World War II, Britain still opposed a Jewish state. The struggle for a Jewish homeland was renewed.

## Chapter Eleven

# Demanding a Home

**W**hen World War II ended, the full horror of Hitler's war against the Jews became known. Six million of our people had been murdered. Half of all the Jews who had lived in Europe were dead.

Some 300,000 Jews who had managed to survive were crowded into miserable camps. They were called "Displaced Persons" and "DP's" because they had no place to go. The word "displaced" hardly describes their terrible situation. Their homes had been destroyed. They had seen parents, children, brothers and sisters tortured and killed.

The great democracies should have offered homes to the victims of such tragedy. Instead, the doors of the western nations stayed almost totally shut, just as they had been when the Nazi death camps were going full blast.

**Dreaming of Palestine**   The Displaced Persons had only one goal: to escape from Europe. Most of them wanted to settle in Eretz Yisrael.

President Harry S. Truman of the United States, was in favor of letting Jewish refugees go to Palestine. He asked Britain to let 100,000 Jews leave the wretched DP camps and settle in the Jewish homeland.

The British refused. They continued to enforce the White Paper of 1939. There would be no increase in immigration.

**The Yishuv Resists**   This British attitude meant that the Displaced Persons would be left homeless. It meant that the Arabs would control Palestine permanently.

The Yishuv had no choice. There was only one way they could reply.

By courageous resistance.

Tel Aviv, 1947: Haganah soldiers defending a Jewish neighborhood.

A turning point came in June 1946. England decided to move every British soldier in the Middle East to Palestine. The Yishuv knew that these soldiers would aid the Arabs, and decided to stop them. In a single night, the Haganah managed to blow up ten of the eleven bridges connecting Palestine to other lands. British troop movements were disrupted.

**The Irgun**　This mission was one of the few cases where the Haganah took offensive action against the British. Most of its work was defensive. The majority of the Jewish population felt that violence, terrorism, and murder were not the right tactics for Jews.

Several groups, however, believed that stronger methods were needed. They broke off from the Haganah to fight in their own way. Of these groups, the most important was the Irgun. It was led by a small, thin man who looked more like a scholar than a revolutionary. He was the man whom the British most wanted to capture and execute.

His name was Menahem Begin.

Menahem Begin, founder of the Irgun and later Prime Minister of Israel.

**Explosion at the King David**   The most famous action of the Irgun took place in Jerusalem in 1946. The site was the beautiful King David Hotel, where the British government had its headquarters.

Irgun men, dressed as Arabs, carried large milk cans into the hotel basement, and left quickly. A young woman telephoned the British with a warning to leave the building. The British paid no attention. According to a later report, a British officer said: "I give the orders here. I don't take orders from Jews."

At 12:37 p.m., time fuses ignited the explosives in the milk cans. The roar was deafening. The southern wing of the hotel seemed to rise in the air before it crashed to the ground in ruins.

Even British headquarters could not be protected from the Jewish passion for freedom.

**A More Powerful Weapon**   The leaders of the Jewish community denounced this as terrorism. They preferred to fight in other ways.

Haganah agents were sent to buy every old ship they could locate. The ships were sailed to ports near the DP (Displaced

The King David Hotel (right) after the explosion of July 22, 1946.

The rebuilt King David hotel, today (below).

When the British seized the Haganah's leaky old ships, they would search for "illegal" refugees and send them back to detention camps in Cyprus.

Persons) camps, secretly loaded with Jewish refugees, and sent on their way to Palestine.

The British did all they could to prevent the loading of the ships, and to catch those that managed to start toward Eretz Yisrael. Few of the ships reached Palestine. Most of the refugees were sent to detention camps on islands in the Mediterranean Sea or the Indian Ocean.

What did this accomplish? It created worldwide sentiment against the British. People reacted with horror at photographs of Englishmen mistreating the helpless survivors of Hitler. The British people turned against their own government. Why were British taxes being used to fight penniless refugees?

**Let the UN Decide**   In April of 1947, the British government gave up. Unable to control the growing violence, unable to deal with the refugee problem, it turned over the responsibility for Palestine to the United Nations.

The UN had been created after World War II to promote international peace. Though only eighteen months old, it now had an extraordinary opportunity to serve the world. It could try to solve the problem of Palestine.

A "United Nations Special Committee on Palestine"—UNSCOP—was created. Its members traveled to the Holy Land to investigate matters.

The Zionists met them eagerly, and explained their needs, plans, and dreams for a Jewish homeland. The Arabs refused to speak to the UNSCOP representatives. They told journalists that a decision to give the Jews land in Palestine would cause riots against Jews who lived in Arab lands.

This attempt to frighten the UNSCOP people failed. It just seemed to prove what the Zionists were saying—that it would be fatal to leave Jews as a minority under Arab control.

**Exodus 1947**   While UNSCOP was doing its work, an old ferryboat named *Exodus 1947*, jammed with 4500 Jewish DP's, sailed for Palestine. It was attacked by a fleet of seven British ships. By ramming and boarding the old boat, then using machine guns and tear gas, the British navy captured the refugee vessel.

What should be done with the refugees? The decision was made by the British Foreign Secretary, Ernest Bevin.

Bevin was the man responsible for Britain's failing policies in the Middle East. He was determined that there would be no increase in Jewish immigration, and no Jewish state. And he was infuriated that Jews kept trying to enter Palestine against his orders.

He decided to make an example of the Jews of *Exodus 1947*. He ordered them sent back to Europe.

After a ghastly voyage, their ship docked in France; but the Jews refused to get off. They insisted that their destination was Palestine. The British then sent them to Germany. The refugees refused again to leave their ship.

Then the British soldiers used clubs to force the Jewish refugees off the ship and back to the land of Adolf Hitler.

This tragedy drove home to UNSCOP the Jewish dilemma.

**What Might Have Been**   If the British and Arabs had approached the subject of Jewish settlement in a reasonable way, the history of the world might have been far happier.

The ship **Exodus 1947,** just after British sailors boarded and took control. They can be identified by their uniforms and white helmets.

In Haifa, alongside the **Exodus 1947,** British troops guard a group of refugee children. The ship's passengers were later sent back to Germany.

If the British had treated Arabs and Jews equally, and forced the Arabs to obey the law, the two groups might have learned to live together peacefully.

If the British had permitted Jews to enter Palestine in reasonable numbers, the English and the Zionists could have joined with the Arabs to build a great land.

On the other hand, if the Arabs had decided to talk to UNSCOP, they might have made some telling points. The refugees from Europe needed homes in Palestine because they weren't allowed into Western countries. The United States, though urging immigration into Eretz Yisrael, kept its own doors locked. During the first eight months of 1946, America admitted only 4767 refugees—barely the number on *Exodus 1947.*

But none of these "ifs" happened. As a result, battle lines were drawn.

Tel Aviv, November 1947. As they heard the results of the United Nations vote, Jews throughout Palestine joined together in huge, outdoor celebrations.

**The Partition Plan**  The UNSCOP report recommended that Palestine be divided into two states: one Arab, one Jewish. Jerusalem, because of its importance to three religions, would be placed under international control. This proposal was known as the "Partition Plan."

The Zionists were disappointed, for they wanted control of their holy city, Jerusalem. They feared the division of the land would be neither fair nor defensible. Still, the plan created a Jewish state and a home for the refugees. They accepted the UNSCOP recommendation.

The Arabs rejected the report entirely.

It was now up to the United Nations to decide what to do.

**UN Debates**  Frantic negotiations took place as Arabs and Zionists looked for support. An Arab victory seemed certain, even though President Truman had pledged American support of the UNSCOP Partition Plan. Then Russia surprised the world by announcing that it, too, would vote in favor of dividing Palestine and creating a Jewish state. For the first time, the United States and USSR would vote together on a major issue.

Nonetheless, there was no guarantee of enough votes to pass the Partition Plan. When the voting began on November 29, 1947, no one knew what the outcome would be.

The nations cast their votes one by one. Most of the European states, many Latin American countries and the members of the British Commonwealth joined the United States and Russia in voting for Partition. All Arab states opposed it. Great Britain did not vote. The final result was thirty-three in favor of dividing Palestine into one Jewish and one Arab state. Thirteen opposed. Ten did not vote. The required two-thirds majority had given its approval.

The UN had said the Jews could have a state in Palestine. It would be up to the Yishuv to make that state a reality.

## SUMMARY

After World War II, the Jewish survivors of Hitler's program against the Jews had nowhere to go. There were 300,000 homeless "Displaced Persons." The democracies of the West would not accept them, and Britain refused to let them into Palestine. The result was a virtual war between the Yishuv and the British. The Irgun's violent tactics included blowing up British headquarters in Jerusalem. The Haganah confronted the British with boatloads of refugees. At last, the British turned the problem of Palestine over to the United Nations. The UN Special Committee on Palestine (UNSCOP), shocked by British cruelty to the refugees on the ship *Exodus 1947*, recommended that Palestine be divided into Arab and Jewish states. The UN accepted this recommendation on November 29, 1947.

## Chapter Twelve

# The Bloody Road to Freedom

**T**wo days after the United Nations voted to create a Jewish state, the Arabs of Palestine went on strike. For three days they brought the country to a halt, while Arab leaders called for death to the Jews. A mob seized clubs and attacked the Jewish Quarter of Jerusalem.

In this way the Arabs told the UN: "Vote as you will. We will keep every inch of Palestine."

**The British Answer the UN**   The British soldiers watched as the rioting Arabs raced toward the Jewish Quarter. It was their duty to maintain order, but they did nothing to stop the attack. Some shot the locks off the doors of Jewish shops to help the Arabs loot and destroy.

Thus, the British told the UN: "We will help the Arabs destroy your plans for a Jewish state."

**The Jews Answer the UN**   Some Jews were determined that Arab rioters would not go unpunished. The Irgun broke into an Arab movie theater and set it on fire, sending a huge pillar of smoke over Jerusalem.

Thus, the Irgun told the UN: "You have given us a state. We will fight for it. We will win."

**Early Arab Victories**   For several months, however, the Jewish position grew worse and worse. Arab forces attacked from every side, destroying and killing. There was no plan to the Arab attacks, but they seemed to show that no Jew was safe.

The Arabs were not able to capture a single Jewish settlement, but they controlled the roads that connected the settlements. By the end of March 1948, the country was cut apart. Settlements in the Negev, to the south, were out of touch with the rest of the

The UN vote enraged many Arabs; some resorted to violence to prevent the formation of a Jewish state. In February, 1948, a bomb wrecked Zion Square in downtown Jerusalem.

The United Nations had promised them a state, but now the Jewish people would have to fight for it. In this picture a Haganah officer trains new recruits in hand-to-hand combat.

The first president of Israel and the thirty-third president of the United States, May 1948. To thank President Truman for his support of the new Jewish state, Weizmann presented him with a Torah scroll.

country. Villages in the north were isolated. Even parts of Jerusalem were unable to communicate.

Many who favored a Jewish state began to doubt that it could survive. The United States suggested that the Jews postpone plans for independence.

**Weizmann and Truman** The Zionists needed President Truman to reaffirm his commitment to Jewish statehood, but he would not even speak with them. They turned to the one man they felt could convince the President—Chaim Weizmann. Weizmann was old, sick, and half-blind, but he responded to their call. He made the long journey from London for an audience with the President.

But Truman had heard enough about Palestine. The White House said there would be no meeting.

Then came one of those strange turns of fate on which history is made.

The President once had a Jewish business partner named Eddie Jacobson. The ex-partners had remained close friends. Weizmann's advisors asked Jacobson for help. He had never been an active Zionist, but he admired Weizmann, and agreed to speak to the President.

The result: Weizmann was secretly admitted to the White House to meet Truman.

Forty-two years earlier, Weizmann had met with Balfour and turned the Englishman into a lifelong Zionist. Again Weizmann's charm, determination, dignity, wisdom, and dedication changed history. When Weizmann arrived, he found a president who was ready to give up the idea of Jewish independence. When Weizmann left, the old Zionist had received a solemn promise that the United States would support the idea of a Jewish state.

**Ben-Gurion's Great Decision**   Yet, could a Jewish state survive? The commander of operations of the Haganah reported, "Perhaps not."

David Ben-Gurion and his advisors listened glumly as General Yigael Yadin continued. Food and supplies could not be driven past the Arab positions on the road to Jerusalem, and the Jewish Quarter was in danger of starvation. Key locations were being handed over to the Arabs by the British.

Yigael Yadin, Commander of Operations for the Haganah in 1948, went on to become a world-famous archaeologist and one of Israel's leading politicians. He died in the summer of 1984.

The Jews had defended themselves bravely against attack, but had not taken the offensive. Yadin insisted on a change of strategy.

Some disagreed. The British would be in Palestine only six more weeks. A Jewish offensive would give them an excuse to stay and fight for the Arabs. Why not wait six weeks?

Yadin would not yield. Food and supplies had to reach Jerusalem. Key locations had to be seized, regardless of the British reaction.

David Ben-Gurion could see only one possible answer. He gave his order.

Attack!

**Turning the Tide**   And attack they did! In April 1948, the Yishuv turned the tide of the undeclared war. The Haganah set out to bring supplies to Jerusalem. The cost was high. Even today you can see the burned remains of armored vehicles that tried to reach the holy city, but were destroyed by the Arabs. They have been left along the roadside as a memorial to those who died in the fighting.

Though many died, others fought on until Jerusalem again had food.

Important locations were captured. The Arabs had planned to use the ancient city of Safed as the center of their campaign. To their dismay, it was taken by the Haganah.

**Death on Both Sides**   Civilians suffered dreadfully—both Jews and Arabs. A convoy of Jewish doctors, nurses, and medical teachers was attacked in Jerusalem. Seventy-seven people were killed.

A group of Jewish extremists attacked the Arab village of Deir Yassin. Two hundred and fifty Arabs were left dead.

The Arabs in Palestine began to fear that if they were captured by Jews, they would be massacred. Arab radio broadcasts warned them to get out of the cities so that Arab armies could destroy the Jews. Misled by fear and their leaders' promises, Arabs began to flee in all directions. When the British left Haifa, for example, tens of thousands of Arabs sped away, leaving behind a nearly empty city for the Zionists to take.

**The Final Vote**   On May 12, 1948, two days before the last British soldiers were to leave Palestine, General Yadin again met

In the spring of 1948, Jewish forces broke through the siege of Jerusalem. This armored vehicle, however, did not survive an Arab ambush. It remains to this day alongside the Tel Aviv-Jerusalem highway, a memorial to those who died for Israeli independence.

with Ben-Gurion and his team. His report was far better than it had been six weeks before. Many key locations were now in Jewish control. The morale of the soldiers was high.

The future still looked grim, however. The armies of five Arab states had massed to attack as soon as the English left. The Zionist army was desperately short of equipment. Some weapons had been purchased in Europe, but the British would not allow them into Palestine. It was by no means certain that the Jewish state could survive until weapons arrived.

Tel Aviv, May 14, 1948. Under a portrait of Theodor Herzl, David Ben-Gurion announces the creation of an independent Jewish state.

Many countries were urging the State of Israel to put off declaring independence. If the Jews would postpone that final step, perhaps a truce with the Arabs could be arranged.

There was a long discussion. At last the vote was taken.

Should the Jews risk everything and declare independence now? Four said no. Six said yes. If one "yes" vote had been changed, the count would have been tied.

The future of Israel was decided by one vote.

**Independence Proclaimed**  On Friday, May 14, 1948, a crowd filled the street outside the Tel Aviv Museum. Inside, at precisely 4:00 p.m. (an hour chosen to avoid the beginning of the Sabbath at sundown), David Ben-Gurion began to read Israel's Proclamation of Independence.

His voice was high-pitched, his delivery undramatic, yet his words were overwhelming. He announced to the world that a new state was being launched in the land that was the birthplace of the Jewish people. It would guarantee equality to all its citizens, and freedom of religion and culture to all.

He concluded: "We extend our hand in peace and neighborliness to all the neighboring states and their peoples, and invite them to cooperate with the independent Jewish nation for the common good of all."

**And That Night ...** The Jews of Tel Aviv celebrated their independence joyfully until late that night. But Ben-Gurion's words had not been heard by the Jews of Jerusalem. Arabs had cut off all electricity, and were preparing to attack.

## SUMMARY

When the United Nations voted to create a Jewish state, the Arabs set off a new wave of violence in Palestine. Many people around the world doubted that a Jewish state could be created. Chaim Weizmann convinced President Truman to support Jewish independence. By going on the offensive the Jews of Palestine improved their military position. Still, no one knew if the State of Israel could survive when, on May 14, 1948, David Ben-Gurion announced the country's independence.

## SPECIAL TOPIC

### A Name for a State

After the dramatic vote to proceed with the creation of a Jewish state, a name for the country had to be chosen.

Different names were suggested. One was "Zion"—a logical name for a state created by a movement called "Zionism." Ben-Gurion preferred another choice. At his urging the new Jewish nation was called **Medinat Yisrael,** the "State of Israel."

## Chapter Thirteen

# The War of Independence

**M**ay 14, 1948. The sun set for the last time over a country named Palestine. At midnight, British control over the land ended. The State of Israel came into being.

Twelve minutes later, President Truman gave official recognition to Israel. The United States became the first country to acknowledge the legitimate claim of the Jewish people to a homeland. Truman had kept his promise to Chaim Weizmann.

And in the few minutes between midnight and President Truman's announcement, five Arab armies began their march to destroy the new Jewish state.

**Five Arab Armies**  It is important to understand that these armies were not made up of Arabs from Palestine. The Palestinian Arabs had little to do with the war against the State of Israel. Left to themselves, they might have accepted the Jewish state. Indeed, the Arabs who did not flee have since lived peacefully as Israeli citizens.

The Arabs who declared war on Israel were from Lebanon, Transjordan, Syria, Iraq, and Egypt.

If these five countries, with their huge resources and modern weapons, had been able to work together, Israel would have been overwhelmed. Fortunately for the Jewish state, the five did not cooperate. Each was out to win power for itself. For example, the Egyptians stopped a ship heading for Transjordan. When they discovered that the ship was filled with ammunition, the Egyptians stole the entire cargo!

**The Syrian Attack**  Still, the Arab countries were so well armed that it seemed that any one of them could have conquered the poorly equipped Israelis.

The Syrians sent a column of 200 tanks into action. The Syrian targets were the kibbutzim at the southern end of the Sea of Galilee, particularly Degania, "the mother of the communal settlements."

The young kibbutzniks had no heavy weapons. The entire Israeli cannon force was rushed north from Jerusalem on a twenty-four hour loan basis. It consisted only of four rusty French howitzers built about 1870! Other than that, the young Jews had only homemade hand grenades.

The Syrian tanks rolled down to the Sea of Galilee, across the flat plain of the Jordan Valley, and crossed the outer limits of Degania. At that moment, the defenders leaped from their trenches and hurled their grenades. The explosions brought the first tanks to a halt.

Moshe Dayan was the commanding officer for the Jordan Valley. He ordered his men to fire the ancient howitzers. The guns were too old to be aimed properly, and one of them would not work at all. But three did fire, making a tremendous noise.

The Syrians feared that their tanks were facing a powerful new weapon. The loud explosions confirmed their worst suspicions; and the Syrians retreated at top speed, all the way back to Syria! Their army was out of the war, thanks to a few hand grenades and some noisy howitzer shells.

**Lebanon and Iraq**  The armies of Lebanon and Iraq scored some early victories. They were minor triumphs, but their forces could have pressed on.

In 1948, in a small village near Gaza, Israeli forces battle for control of the Negev.

Instead, the Lebanese and Iraqis decided to play safe. They simply didn't want to fight. Proof of their attitude was found when dead Iraqi soldiers were discovered chained to their guns. Their officers had obviously been afraid that the soldiers would throw away their weapons and run.

**Egypt**   The Egyptian army was a different matter. While the Israelis were celebrating independence on May 14, the Egyptians were loading planes with bombs. In the early hours of the next morning, as Ben-Gurion was speaking on the radio to the people of America, he included a dramatic announcement. The explosions which could be clearly heard on the radio were the first bombs to be dropped on the Jewish state as its War of Independence began.

The Egyptians met fierce resistance from the kibbutzim of the south. Nonetheless, within two weeks the Egyptian army was only sixteen miles from Tel Aviv. The city had a population of a quarter million Jews. To the Egyptians it seemed an easy prey. To General Yadin, it was a city that could not be allowed to fall.

Yadin decided to risk everything on a daring night attack on the rear of the Egyptian army. The Jewish forces numbered barely half those of the invaders, and had much inferior weapons. Nevertheless, their unexpected arrival in the darkness threw the Egyptians into a panic. They fled wildly. Tel Aviv was saved.

**Transjordan—and Jerusalem**   The heaviest fighting of the war was for Jerusalem. The UN had declared that the city would be under international control, but no one in the Middle East took that seriously. Transjordan was determined to capture the city. The Israelis were just as determined to make it part of the Jewish state.

In 1948, Jerusalem was not a large city, but it was divided in three parts. East Jerusalem was Arab. West Jerusalem, the New City, was Jewish. The Old City, surrounded by walls, was a mixture. The Jewish inhabitants of the Old City were Orthodox, living in small stone houses surrounded by dozens of yeshivot, synagogues, and sacred sites.

The first battle was for the Old City. The Arab Legion, armed and commanded by British officers, was able to overcome the valiant Jewish defense. Those Jews who survived the siege were sent to West Jerusalem or to prisoner-of-war camps. The Old City was to remain in Jordanian hands until the Six Day War of 1967.

**The Fight for the New City**   West Jerusalem was all Jewish, but it was ringed by Arab forces. Conditions inside were dreadful. The only road to the city passed a British police station at Latrun, occupied by well-armed Arabs. Direct attacks on it resulted only in bloody losses for the Israelis. This left the 50,000 Jews of Jerusalem without food, water, or supplies. The only material coming into the city arrived in a tiny plane from Tel Aviv that could carry one barrel of flour or ammunition per flight. Still the starving Jews held out.

Time was running out. The Arabs, realizing that the expected easy victory could turn into disaster, called for a truce to take effect June 11. When the truce began, land controlled by the Arabs would remain in Arab control. If the new Israeli army could not free Jerusalem, the Jews would be forced out and the whole city would be seized by Transjordan.

**A Road to Victory**   Once again the Israelis took a desperate gamble. The commander of the Jerusalem campaign was an American, Colonel David Marcus. He discovered a footpath in the hills around Latrun, out of sight of the Arab machine guns. If that path could be widened, trucks with supplies might be able to reach Jerusalem.

It was a last chance. Hundreds of laborers were rushed from Tel Aviv. Day and night they raced against time, laboring in the fiercest heat.

Just two nights before the ceasefire, the first trucks began the dangerous journey over the makeshift road. Slowly, carefully, they strained up the mountain. At last they reached their goal: Jerusalem. Food, water, and ammunition arrived. The city was saved.

The ceasefire took effect. Yet even this was colored with tragedy. In the last minutes before the truce, a Jewish sentry fired at a man in the foggy night, a man who seemed not to know the evening's password. The soldier had made a tragic mistake. The man he killed was the American who had saved Jerusalem, Colonel David Marcus.

**The War Ends**   The truce was welcomed by both sides. The Israelis, however, had far more than the Arabs to gain from it. The weapons which had been purchased for Israel and stored in Europe during British rule were now rushed to the country. Jews who had been waiting to enter Eretz Yisrael arrived by the thousands.

The funeral of Colonel David Marcus, June 1948.

When the truce ended, the Israelis were ready with well-armed soldiers. Sudden attacks drove the Egyptians from the Negev. The Lebanese were driven back to the old border in the north. By the time a new truce was declared, Israel was in possession of 21 percent more land than had originally been assigned to it by the United Nations Partition plan.

**Sorrow and Victory**   The Israeli War of Independence was relatively short. It lasted just over a year, from December 1947 to January 1949, and there were only sixty days of fighting. Even so, the Jewish losses were staggering: 7,000 killed, 1 percent of Israel's small population. (By comparison, the United States during four years of fighting in World War II lost three-tenths of 1 percent of its people.)

Despite these sorrows, the Israeli victory seemed a miracle. The tiny Jewish nation had triumphed over the combined armies

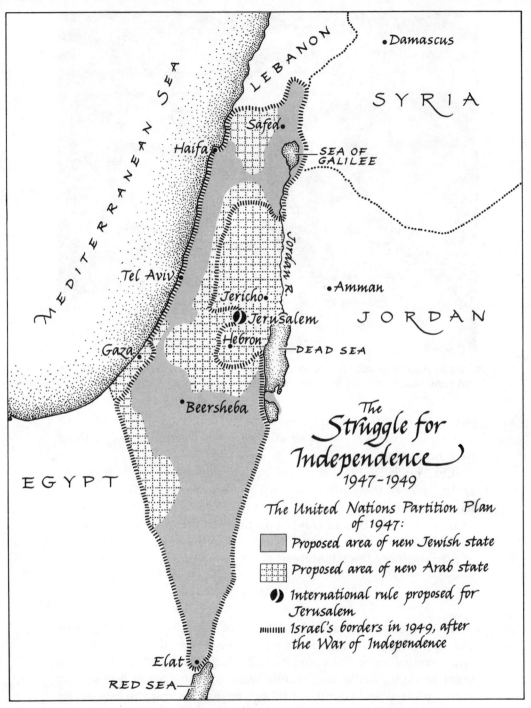

Map labels:
MEDITERRANEAN SEA
LEBANON
•Damascus
SYRIA
Safed•
Haifa•
SEA OF GALILEE
Jordan R.
Tel Aviv•
Jericho•
•Amman
Jerusalem
JORDAN
Hebron•
Gaza•
DEAD SEA
•Beersheba
EGYPT
Elat•
RED SEA

The
Struggle for
Independence
1947-1949

The United Nations Partition Plan
of 1947:

Proposed area of new Jewish state

Proposed area of new Arab state

International rule proposed for
Jerusalem

Israel's borders in 1949, after
the War of Independence

This map shows the Partition Plan put forward by the United Nations in
November of 1947. Palestine was to be divided into two nations, one Jewish,
and one Arab; Jerusalem would have been under international control. But
the Arabs did not accept the plan, and attacked. When the War of Independence was over, the new State of Israel contained more land than the United
Nations had promised. Jerusalem became a divided city, the western section
in Israeli hands and the eastern section controlled by Jordan.

A bitter price was paid for victory, but Israelis, and Jews around the world, can now march proudly on Israel's Independence Day.

of the Arab world. For the first time in 2000 years, Jews had been victorious in a war. Most of all, the Jews were masters in their own homeland.

On March 11, 1949, the blue-and-white Israeli flag was raised at the plaza of the United Nations in New York City. The State of Israel was officially a member of the family of nations. Only four years earlier, the Star of David had marked the millions who were murdered by Nazi Germany. Now it was the emblem on the flag of a proud new Jewish state.

### SUMMARY

Five Arab armies attacked the State of Israel within minutes of the end of British rule. Fortunately for Israel, the efforts of the Arab armies were not coordinated. Many Arab soldiers did not want to fight, while the Israelis were fighting for survival. The Israeli victory was costly, with high casualties and the loss of the Old City in Jerusalem to the Arabs. Nevertheless, daring strategy and courageous fighting brought victory to the ill-equipped Israelis. For the first time in 2000 years, the Jews were rulers in their own homeland.

PART FOUR
# The State of Israel

## Chapter Fourteen

# Coming Home

**I**magine what it would be like if the number of children in your school suddenly doubled. There would be a mad scramble for desks, for books, for pencils and paper.

Now imagine that the new children were all foreigners. They came from all over the world and spoke dozens of different languages.

And to make things worse, imagine that some were more advanced in their studies than you, while others couldn't even read or write.

An impossible situation? It could never be made to work?

Yet something very much like that happened in Israel. In less than five years, the Jewish population of the new country doubled. The immigrants came from all over the world, from every level of society and education.

**The Call to Return**   The British had severely limited Jewish immigration to Palestine. One of the first acts of the new State of Israel was to open the doors of the Promised Land to every Jew. The call rang out: "Israel is a reality. Come home."

From Europe, where those who had survived the Nazis were imprisoned in Displaced Person camps, Jews poured out. Sick, homeless, penniless, they made their way to their homeland.

In only nineteen months, Israel welcomed 340,000 Jewish immigrants. This was almost three times the number admitted by the British during the previous nine years.

**From the Muslim World**   The victims of Hitler had captured world attention. But there was another Jewish world that had been largely forgotten. Between one and a half and two million Jews lived in Muslim lands.

Many of these Jewish communities were very ancient. Jews

had first settled in places like Iraq when the Temple of Solomon was destroyed in 586 B.C.E. When the Muslims took over the countries twelve centuries later, they often persecuted the Jews. Conditions became even worse after 1948, when Israel defeated the Arab armies. Other Arabs wanted revenge.

The Jews in the Muslim world were desperate to move to Israel.

**Operation: Magic Carpet**  One of the first groups came from Yemen.

Yemen is a country on the southwest of the Arabian Peninsula. Jews had lived there since ancient times, but over the centuries had been forced into terrible poverty. When they heard

The **Galila,** one of the first ships to carry Jewish refugees to the new Jewish state, pulls into the port of Haifa with some 1500 ''Displaced Persons'' on board. Thousands more crowd the dock to welcome the new immigrants.

Operation: Magic Carpet. Yemenite Jews, most of them in an airplane for the first time in their lives, on their way to Israel.

that a Jewish state had been created, nothing would stop them from returning to Eretz Yisrael.

The nearest airport was 200 miles away at Aden. The Yemenites picked up their few possessions and started to walk. Along the way they were looted and abused by the Arabs. They reached Aden, exhausted and all but starved. Israel and the world Jewish community made plans to fly them to the Promised Land.

The project was called "Operation: Magic Carpet." It would have been easy if magic carpets had been available! Instead, crowded planes flew back and forth between Israel and the Yemenite refugee camps for over a year, around the clock.

The Yemenite Jews had never seen airplanes, but were not frightened by them. In the Book of Isaiah (40:31), God promised that His children would return to Zion "with wings, as eagles." Here were the giant wings to fulfill God's promise!

The fact that they had faith, however, did not mean that the Yemenites knew how to behave in planes. When mealtime arrived, one man started to cook his meal by making a fire on the floor of the passenger section.

Nevertheless, the whole move was made without accident.

The entire Jewish community of Yemen—45,000 people—arrived safely in Israel.

**Operation: Ali Baba** The rescue of Yemenite Jewry was a dress rehearsal for "Operation: Ali Baba," in which almost three times as many Jews were rescued from Iraq.

The modern state of Iraq is located in one of the centers of ancient civilization. The city of Ur, where Abraham was born, was located there. It is the place in which the Babylonian Talmud, the great treasurehouse of Jewish law and lore, was completed.

Periods of peace for the Iraqi Jews alternated with periods of oppression. In 1950 the Jewish community was fairly prosperous, but it was also in danger. Iraq was an Arab state at war with Israel. Any Jew who expressed sympathy for Israel was in trouble with the government. Any Jew who tried to leave Iraq and go to Israel was executed.

Then an Arab official had a wickedly clever idea. Why not let the Jews leave for Israel? The government would promise to take good care of Jewish property. Once the Jews were gone, the government could steal everything they had left behind!

This is exactly what happened. The Jews lost an enormous amount of property, but it was a good exchange. In Israel, they found safety and freedom. Only 4000 Jews chose to stay in Iraq. There were 121,000 others who were happy to find new lives in the State of Israel.

**Tent Cities** The immigrants poured in from every Muslim land. They came from Turkey, from Africa, from forgotten little communities in Iran and Afghanistan. Through the centuries, they had kept their Jewish identity. Now they could come home.

"Home" at first meant a leaky tent. It was impossible for the Israeli government to create proper houses for so many people in such a short time. The immigrants were crowded into tent cities, called *maabarot*.

Imagine a man who has survived the Nazi death camps. His health is poor. He is alone, with few if any of his family still alive. He has come to Israel—and finds himself living with Jews who have never seen a flush toilet.

He stares at these strange people, who perhaps come from caves in Morocco.

They stare back at him. They know nothing of his language or

A **maabarah,** or tent city, in 1952.

his background. They are told he is a Jew, but his traditions are different from theirs. The way he cooks his food seems strange and disgusting.

The government worked as hard as it could to move the immigrants into new homes. In only ten years, they had succeeded. The last of the tent cities disappeared by 1958. All over the country there were prosperous new villages and farms, often built by new immigrants.

**Problems Remain** More than housing was needed for those who came from less developed countries—people who could not read or write, or work in any modern craft. They had no idea of how to live in a world of science and machines. In many cases, they did not want to learn. They simply wanted to practice their old traditions in Eretz Yisrael.

Well-educated people had problems, too. They wanted to find suitable jobs. In the 1970s, a large number of well-trained Jews came from Russia. They wanted to have work as interesting and homes as comfortable as they had left behind.

Before long, the country was divided into two societies. On the one hand were Western Jews, mostly of European background, who had education, good jobs, and power. On the other hand, the Eastern Jews, mostly from Muslim lands, had little.

**Finding Solutions** You might think that the Jews of European background would do everything to keep power in their own hands, particularly since the Oriental Jews became a majority of the population. Instead, the Europeans work hard to help their fellow Jews become full partners in Israeli society.

All immigrants to Israel are given courses in Hebrew. The less-educated also receive special training to help them adjust to life in a modern state. In the schools, the disadvantaged children are given special courses. Extra scholarships are arranged for them. Sometimes their parents receive funds so that they can afford to let their older children stay in school instead of going to work.

It will take a generation or two for this to have its full effect, but already the two societies are merging. One of every five marriages unites Jews of different backgrounds. It is hoped that the best of each Jewish tradition will be preserved, even as the young people work to build a united Israel.

Immigrants leaving Italy in 1949, bound for the Promised Land.

Russian Jews arriving at Ben Gurion Airport.

The Jews now have a land of their own, but they have not forgotten the pain of other "Displaced Persons." During the late 1970's, Israel was one of the few countries in the world to welcome the "boat people," refugees from war-torn Southeast Asia.

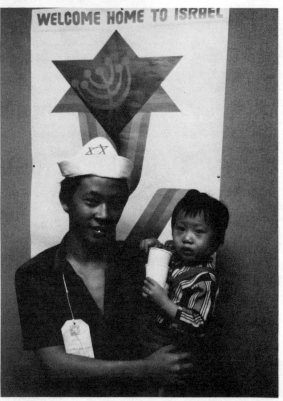

114    THE STATE OF ISRAEL

An Israeli girl teaches Hebrew to a young Ethiopian immigrant. For centuries, the Jews of Ethiopia lived in an isolated community, cut off from the Jewish world. Most of them now want to come to Israel, but the journey is long and difficult. Because the Ethiopian government does not want to let them go, they must leave in secret, walking hundreds of miles until they cross the Sudanese border. In 1984, a terrible drought brought starvation and death to this part of the world. The Israeli government launched an emergency rescue mission, "Operation Moses." By the end of the year Operation Moses had brought thousands of Ethiopian Jews to a new home, and safety, in Israel.

## SUMMARY

As soon as Israel was created, the country was opened to Jewish immigration. Europeans who had been victims of the Nazis and who, after World War II, had been locked up in Displaced Person camps, were the first to pour into the new state. They were followed by a larger number of refugees from Muslim lands. In time, the Jews from Muslim lands became more than half the population of Israel. Many came from less developed lands and had difficulty becoming full members of Israeli society. Strong efforts are being made to help them improve their lives.

## Chapter Fifteen

# The Fight for Survival

**N**o nation should be forced to go to war time and time again. No nation should be surrounded by neighbors who dream of its destruction.

No nation should have to explain, year after year, that it has the right to live, and to defend itself.

Yet Israel has had to do all these things.

**Many Accomplishments**  Surrounded by nations that seek to destroy it, Israel has been forced to build one of the finest armies in the world. Most of its Jewish citizens, boys and girls, men and women, have military training. In the first thiry-four years of the country's history, they have had to fight five major wars.

It is easy to think of Israel as a society of soldiers. What is remarkable, however, is what the Israelis have accomplished despite their military needs. They have built farms, even in the desert. They have restored forests. They have built museums and schools and theatres. They have given homes to Jews from every continent. They have built the only democracy in the Middle East.

**After Independence**  The Israeli War of Independence ended in clear victory for the new Jewish state. Most people expected that the war would be followed by peace treaties between Israel and the Arab states.

It was not to be.

For more than a generation, every Arab leader had said that Zionists were villains. No Arab leader had the courage to change. Each was afraid to appear "soft" by signing a peace treaty with the Israelis. Those who considered making peace, such as King Abdullah of Jordan, were assassinated by other Arabs.

The pattern was set. The Arabs were not able to fight a successful war, but they would not permit peace.

Nearly all young Israelis serve in their country's armed forces. Here a soldier stands guard near the Dead Sea.

**Nasser**   It was only a matter of time before an Arab leader would start a new war. The man was an army officer who had seized control of Egypt: Colonel Gamal Abdul Nasser.

Nasser had grand dreams. He wanted Egypt to be the leader of the Arab states. He decided the way to gain Arab support was to lead the campaign against Israel. His plan was to destroy the Jewish state by cutting off its lifelines to the rest of the world.

**A Dangerous Location**   A glance at a map will show you how easy it seemed to do this.

Imagine that you had a business in Israel. How would you bring supplies into the country?

You cannot bring in anything by land. Every land route crosses an Arab country which would seize any product addressed to Israel.

You can bring supplies by air, but air freight is very expensive.

The best way to bring in goods is by sea. Products from Europe can come without difficulty through the Mediterranean Sea. Goods from the Far East, however, must pass through two narrow waterways. One is the Strait of Tiran, which lies between Saudi Arabia and Egypt. The other is the Suez Canal, which is completely inside Egyptian territory.

**Choking Israel**   In 1956, Nasser announced that he was cutting off both these routes to Israel. He was putting guns on the islands in the Strait of Tiran, and he would destroy any ship going to or from Israel.

In addition, he was taking control of the Suez Canal from the French and English, who had built and operated it.

**The Suez Campaign**   France and England wanted to keep control of the Suez Canal. Israel needed to open its shipping routes. The three decided to work together.

On October 29, 1956, the three countries launched a joint attack on Egypt. The fighting took only one hundred hours. The world was surprised by the short, sudden war. But it was even more surprised at the results.

The combined armies of France and England had failed to seize the Suez Canal. Israel, however, had conquered the entire Sinai Peninsula.

Eventually world pressure forced Israel to return the land to Egypt; but the Jewish state gained a great deal in exchange. A United Nations army unit was established to guard the Israel-Egypt border, and to guarantee that all ships could pass safely through the Suez Canal and the Strait of Tiran.

**A Worse Crisis**   For ten years there was peace. Nasser felt that he had to take new action against Israel if he was to remain a leader of the Arab world. He ordered the United Nations Emergency Force to leave the area, and again blockaded the Strait of Tiran.

At the Strait of Tiran, an Israeli soldier stands next to captured Egyptian artillery.

Amazingly enough, the United Nations forces left the area immediately. When they were most needed, they hurried away. As Israel's Foreign Minister, Abba Eban, asked: "What is the use of a United Nations presence if it is, in effect, an umbrella which is taken away as soon as it begins to rain?"

The world stood in terror before Nasser. The United States or Britain might have defied him by sending a ship to Israel through the Strait of Tiran. They did not. France stopped sending weapons to Israel.

Israel was alone.

**The Six Day War** On June 5, 1967, Israel gave its answer. Its forces broke through the Egyptian front lines.

This was the beginning of the "Six Day War." Actually, the war was won in the first six hours, when Israel's pilots destroyed Egypt's entire air force.

Even as his troops were being battered, Nasser announced great victories. Syria and Jordan, eager to join in what they believed was a massacre of the Jews, attacked Israel. Within a week they, too, were defeated.

The Israeli triumph was complete. The Sinai Peninsula was again under Israel's control. The mountains in northeast Israel, the Golan Heights, from which Syrian soldiers had fired upon

Jewish farm settlements, were captured by Israel's soldiers. The entire area west of the Jordan River was retaken.

The most thrilling victory was the capture of the Old City of Jerusalem. Since 1948 it had been under the control of Jordan. Jews had not been permitted to enter. Now Jews could again pray at the Western Wall of the Jerusalem Temple, the most sacred site of Jewish tradition.

Jews all over the world looked for a word to describe what had happened. The best they could say was, "A miracle."

**The Yom Kippur War**   Again there was a period of peace. Nasser died in 1970, and a little-known follower of his became president of Egypt. His name was Anwar Sadat.

On Yom Kippur of 1973, the Israelis went to their synagogues to worship. On that holiest of days, Egypt and Syria launched surprise attacks.

Israeli soldiers dashed from their prayers to their battle stations, but the Arabs had gained precious time by attacking first. It took Israel three weeks to organize, stop the Arab advance, and counterattack.

When the shooting stopped, the Israeli forces had again performed the impossible. They had smashed the Egyptian lines and crossed the Suez Canal, surrounding and trapping 20,000 Egyptian soldiers. The Israelis were only sixty miles from Cairo, the capital of Egypt, and were even closer to Damascus, the capital of Syria.

Yet it was not a happy victory. The Jewish state paid a terrible price in human life for being caught unprepared. Two thousand Jewish soldiers fell in battle. Almost every Israeli lost a friend or relative in the Yom Kippur War.

**War Yields Peace**   Israel's losses were heavy. Still, by normal standards, the Arabs had again suffered a staggering defeat.

But normal standards never apply in the Middle East. Anwar Sadat felt he had restored "Arab honor" because in this war, unlike the others, Arabs had fought bravely and well.

Having led the Egyptians in what he believed was a successful war, Sadat was ready to lead them to peace. In 1977, at the invitation of the Prime Minister of Israel, he flew to Israel to speak to the Knesset, Israel's Parliament.

The world stood in awe. Anwar Sadat was a former Nazi sympathizer. The Prime Minister of Israel was Menahem Begin,

First steps toward peace: Moshe Dayan, Anwar Sadat, and Menahem Begin at a ceremonial dinner in Jersualem.

former leader of the Jewish terrorist organization (the Irgun). Now the two were standing together in Jerusalem, pledging that their nations would never again battle each other.

The road to peace was not simple. A year and a half passed before Begin and Sadat, with the help and pressure of American President Jimmy Carter, signed the peace treaty known as the Camp David Agreement. In 1982, the entire Sinai was returned to Egypt, as stated in the agreement.

Hesitantly, Egypt and Israel were trying to work together.

**Arab Opposition** Other Arab leaders denounced the peace treaty. The statement that Israel had a right to exist was viewed by them as treason. In October 1981, fanatic Arabs murdered President Sadat.

It was all very strange. Sadat was assassinated while watching a parade honoring the eighth anniversary of the Yom Kippur War. He was murdered by Arabs, for whose honor he had launched that war. He was mourned by Israelis, who had lost so much in that war.

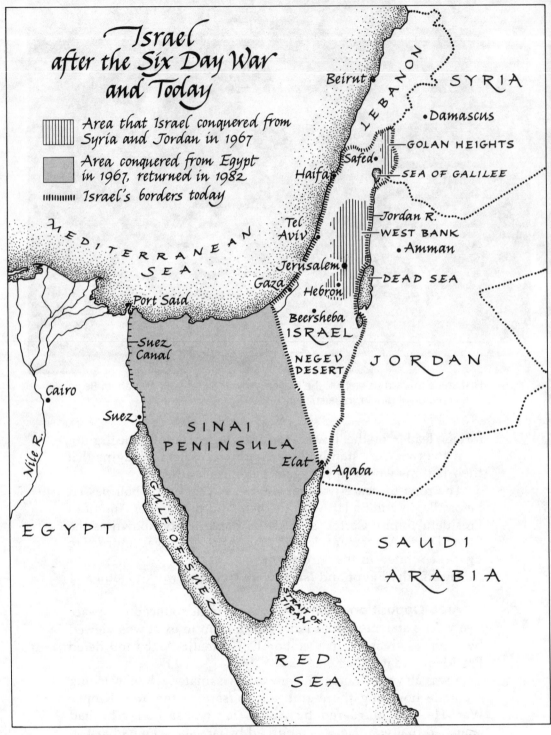

Israel
after the Six Day War
and Today

Area that Israel conquered from
Syria and Jordan in 1967

Area conquered from Egypt
in 1967, returned in 1982

Israel's borders today

MEDITERRANEAN
SEA

Beirut

SYRIA

LEBANON

Damascus

GOLAN HEIGHTS

Safed

SEA OF GALILEE

Haifa

Tel
Aviv

Jordan R.

WEST BANK

Amman

Jerusalem

Gaza

Hebron

DEAD SEA

Port Said

Beersheba

ISRAEL

Suez
Canal

NEGEV
DESERT

JORDAN

Cairo

Suez

SINAI
PENINSULA

Elat

Aqaba

Nile R.

GULF OF SUEZ

EGYPT

SAUDI

ARABIA

STRAIT OF TIRAN

RED
SEA

During the Six Day War of 1967 Israel captured territory from Egypt, Jordan,
and Syria. All of Jerusalem, including the Old City and the Western Wall,
came under Israeli control. After signing a 1979 peace agreement with Egypt,
Israel gave up the Sinai Peninsula, but kept the other areas conquered in
1967.

**Crisis in Lebanon**   The peace treaty which Sadat signed remained in effect after his death. Northern Israel, however, was being attacked by Palestinian terrorists who had settled in—and terrorized—the country of Lebanon. In June 1982, Israeli troops entered Lebanon and crushed the Palestinian and Syrian forces.

The Lebanese people cheered Israel for freeing them from the Palestinian terrorists. Once the fighting was over, however, the Lebanese government—under pressure from other Arab states—asked the Israelis to leave. Lebanon had been so shattered in the years of Palestinian occupation that the government was not strong enough to control the country. Israel did not want to withdraw only to have the terrorists return.

This problem has not been resolved.

**The Future**   No one can predict the future of the Middle East. It is clear that the Arabs have gained nothing by maintaining a state of war with Israel. Everyone would profit by joining hands, and rebuilding the region in peace.

Whether any nation will join Egypt in recognizing this fact remains to be seen.

### SUMMARY

Israel has fought five major wars:
    1947–49—The Israeli War of Independence.
    1956—The Suez Campaign.
    1967—The Six Day War.
    1973—The Yom Kippur War.
    1982—The Drive Into Lebanon.
Although Israel won each war, the cost to the country was high. Strangely enough, Anwar Sadat, the man who launched the bloody Yom Kippur War, was the first Arab to sign a peace treaty with Israel.

### SPECIAL TOPIC

#### The West Bank

Since the Six Day War, the government of Israel has encouraged Jews to settle in the area west of the Jordan River that once was controlled by Jordan. This area is often called the "West Bank," though Jews who settle there prefer the Biblical names of "Samaria" and "Judea."

There are two reasons for these new Jewish settlements.

First, it is argued, Jews lived there for many centuries until they were driven out in the Arab riots of the 1920s and 1930s. Jordan seized the land in defiance of the United Nations. Now that Israel controls the area, why should it prevent Jews from living in their traditional homeland?

Second, it is felt that Jewish settlements provide an excellent line of defense against future attacks from Jordan.

Whenever possible, the Jews settle on empty, uncultivated land. Sometimes, however, the best places for defense have been places that had been owned by Arabs. The government has taken these lands in the interest of national defense.

Israelis freely debate whether or not this is a wise policy. Is it better to have a strong line of defense or peace with the local Arabs? The democratic tradition of Israel is so strong that not only Jews argue these questions. Arabs are allowed to hold demonstrations, and even to take the Israeli government to court to defend their legal rights.

The landscape of the area known as the West Bank has changed in recent years. Arab villages like this one (left) have been joined by new Jewish settlements (right). But many Israelis protest (below) that these new settlements are an obstacle to peace.

## Chapter Sixteen

# A Different Democracy

In America, we take freedom for granted. We expect to be allowed to say what we wish. We expect that every adult will be permitted to vote.

In the Middle East, democracy is almost unknown. Every state except one is ruled by some sort of dictator. He may be a king, or a general, or a "president" who is elected without any real opponent.

The only country in the Middle East that is a true democracy is the State of Israel.

**Similarities to America** All citizens of Israel enjoy free speech, freedom of the press, and freedom of religion. They vote for the representatives who form the government. In Israel, every citizen over eighteen years of age may vote in national elections.

In these ways, democracy in Israel is similar to that of the United States. In other ways, the two systems are different.

**Some Differences** One difference is that the United States Congress is made up of two lawmaking bodies—the Senate and the House of Representatives. Israel has only one body of 120 lawmakers. They are elected, usually for four-year terms, to a Parliament, called the Knesset. (This is a Hebrew word that means "assembly.") They meet in the beautiful Knesset building in Jerusalem.

In America we have two major political parties, the Democrats and the Republicans. There are also smaller parties that run candidates. In the voting for any office, only one party can win. If you vote for a Democrat and the Republican receives more votes, you lose completely. You don't get a "little bit" of Democrat representation. You get none at all.

The Israelis didn't think this was a good arrangement. From

the early days of the Zionist Congresses, effort was made to give every opinion some representation. That aim was carried over into the structure of the Israeli government.

**Preparing for Elections**   Israel has many small parties, each representing a point of view. Before a national election, each party makes a list of its candidates. The most important person in the party is number 1 on the list. The second most important is number 2, and so on.

The people of Israel then vote for the party of their choice. In theory, they are not voting for individual candidates as much as they are voting for the party which represents their ideas.

The votes are counted. Each party has received some percentage of the votes. It receives the same percentage of seats in the Knesset.

**Forming a Government**   Since there are 120 seats in the Knesset, 61 seats are needed for a majority.

An Arab woman casts her vote in a local election. All Israeli citizens have the right to vote.

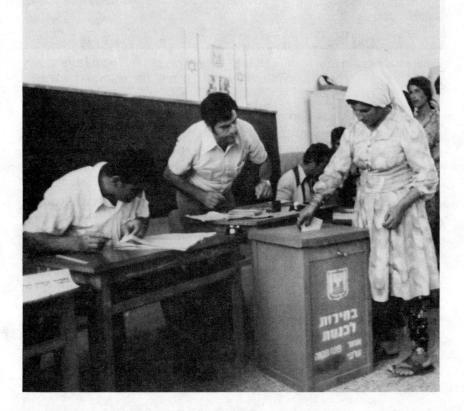

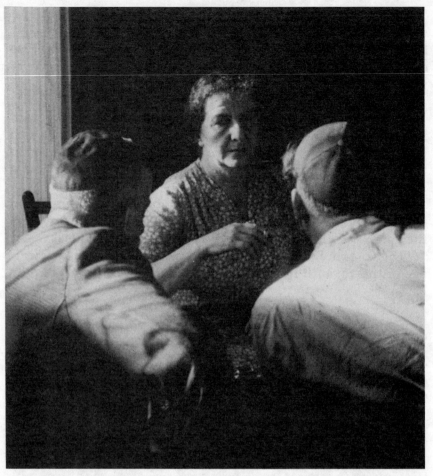

A necessary skill in Israeli politics is the ability to negotiate. This picture shows Golda Meir in consultation with members of one of the religious parties.

Let us say that, in an election, Party A receives the most votes, but wins only forty-eight seats. If it stands alone, it will never win. (That has always been the situation in Israeli elections. There are over twenty parties, and no party has ever won a majority.)

It is now the job of the leader of Party A to meet with leaders of other parties and come to an agreement to vote together. This is called "forming a government." He must bargain to win the cooperation of the others. He may have to give up some of what his party wants, and give the smaller parties some of what they want. This process of negotiation can be long and difficult.

**Choosing Partners**  The leader of Party A looks at the election results. Which party should he talk to first? He could work with Party B, which (we shall say) came in second with thirty seats. Together the two parties would have an overwhelming majority.

But should he do that? He doesn't need all the votes of Party B. He needs only a few votes for a majority. Furthermore, the leader of Party B is his political rival. Cooperation would give him more power and influence.

No, says the leader of Party A. Let's look elsewhere. I need only thirteen votes for a majority. Party C has eighteen, just enough for a little margin of safety. The party is too small to be a real rival. It will be so grateful to be in the government, it won't ask for many favors.

He calls on the leader of Party C. The two bargain. When they reach an agreement, they announce that they have formed a government. The leader of Party A becomes "Prime Minister"—the leader of the country.

**True-Life Problems**  This system has the advantage of giving small parties representation. It has the disadvantage of giving small parties more power than they are entitled to when the leading party needs their votes to gain a majority.

These small parties include those that believe in an extreme Orthodox interpretation of Judaism. They have insisted on control of Jewish religious life in Israel as their condition for voting with the government. As a result, the extreme Orthodox Jews control marriages, divorces, and burials.

This has disturbed some Orthodox Jews in America, who regard the Orthodox officials in Israel as too rigid in their interpretation of Judaism. For Israelis who are not religious, or who are Conservative or Reform Jews, the situation can present problems. To be married, for example, they must have an Orthodox wedding, or else must leave the country and have their wedding elsewhere before returning.

In short, Israel is a democracy where there is freedom of religion. All faiths recognized by the Israeli Ministry of Religion have full control over matters of marriage, divorce and burial, for their followers.

Unfortunately, Conservative and Reform rabbis have not been recognized by the Ministry of Religion, and do not have the same privileges as Orthodox rabbis. The growing number of Conservative and Reform congregations are struggling to obtain equal recognition.

# SUMMARY

Israel is the only country in the Middle East that is a democracy. The country elects representatives to its parliament, the Knesset. Each party receives a percentage of the 120 seats in the Knesset equal to the percentage of the vote it receives. Since no party has ever received a majority, the leading party must bargain for support from other parties. In practice, this has given small parties a larger voice in government than they would otherwise have. The extreme Orthodox parties have used this to keep more liberal forms of Judaism from gaining official recognition.

## SPECIAL TOPIC

### A Gallery of Israel's Leaders

**David Ben-Gurion** (1886–1973), the first prime minister of Israel. After leading the struggle to create a Jewish state, he had the honor of proclaiming the country's independence on May 14, 1948. He then served as prime minister for most of its first fourteen years. During his term of office the country fought and won two wars, while at the same time absorbing an enormous number of new immigrants.

**Chaim Weizmann** (1874–1952), the great Zionist leader who convinced the British to issue the Balfour Declaration. This was the first official statement by any nation that Jews had a right to a homeland in Palestine. Weizmann served as Israel's first president until his death in 1952.

**Golda Meir** (1898–1978), born in Russia and raised in Milwaukee. She settled in Palestine and became a dynamic member of the Zionist movement. Later she served as Israel's first ambassador to the Soviet Union. As prime minister from 1969 to 1974, she became one of Israel's most popular leaders, and was known and admired throughout the world.

**Menahem Begin** (born 1913), the leader of the Irgun. He took command of this underground army soon after his arrival in Palestine, directing it in its attempt to force the British out of the country. As prime minister from 1977 to 1983, he signed the first peace treaty between Israel and an Arab state.

**Rabbi Abraham Isaac Kook** (1865–1935), first chief rabbi of Palestine after British rule began in 1921. Though a deeply religious Jew, he taught respect for all types of belief. He felt that non-Orthodox Jews were also serving God by rebuilding the Jewish homeland. Still, he felt that a Jewish state could not be truly successful or complete unless it was guided by the spiritual teachings of Judaism.

## Chapter Seventeen

# Israelis and Arabs

Almost every day there is something in the news about Israelis and Arabs. Their relationship is a matter of major concern to the world. Every dispute in the Middle East may endanger the supply of oil to other countries.

It is important to understand what is really going on between the Arabs and Jews. That is very difficult, however, because the Arabs specialize in a propaganda technique known as "The Big Lie."

**The Big Lie**  The Big Lie was a technique introduced by Hitler. It is: if you say a big enough lie loud enough, and often enough, people will come to believe it.

Hitler used the Big Lie against the Jews. He told the German people that Jews were terrible animals, plotting to destroy the country.

When enough Germans believed that Jews were a threat to them, Hitler was able to launch his plan to exterminate the Jewish people.

**The Arab Big Lie**  The Arabs, some of whom cooperated with the Nazis in World War II, learned the Big Lie technique. The Arab Big Lie goes like this: "Zionist Jews hate all other races, especially the Arabs. They have taken away the rights of Arabs whenever they could. The Arabs who live in the West Bank lands have a right to a state of their own. Only when these Palestinians have a state can there be peace in the Middle East."

Impressive sounding? Do you find yourself saying, "There must be some truth in that"?

There is none. The whole paragraph is a complete lie. Let's examine it.

**The UN's Lie** "Zionists are racists," say the Arabs. This is a terrible accusation, but the United Nations says it is true. In 1975, the Arabs were able to control enough votes in the UN to pass a resolution condemning Zionism as a form of racism.

But if the UN passed 1000 such resolutions, they would still all be lies.

Zionism is the political movement to create a Jewish homeland. In forming the Jewish state, the Zionists deliberately created a democracy in which all groups are free and equal. Many religions are practiced in Israel in total freedom. Many racial groups live in Israel as equals. Israel was also particularly helpful to the new black states of Africa.

Arabs have lived in peace in Israel ever since the state was founded. The Arabs have representatives in the Knesset. When the city of Jerusalem was reunified after the Six Day War, all the Arabs in the city were allowed to become citizens of Israel.

Arabs have shared in Israel's prosperity. New homes like these are a familiar sight in Arab villages throughout Israel.

Arab women and children at a government health clinic.

**Taking Away Arab Rights?** "The Zionists take away Arab rights," say the Arab nations. It is a lie.

The Arabs in Palestine had few rights until they came under Israeli rule. Even today, Arabs in Arab states have few rights. They have no freedom of speech or press. They cannot go to court to complain against government injustice. Women generally cannot vote.

All these rights are given to the Arabs by Israel. An Arab has far more rights in Israel than he does in any Arab state.

**A West Bank State?** The Arabs demand an independent Arab state on the West Bank, the land west of the Jordan River that was captured by Israel during the Six Day War.

What is never made clear is why this tiny territory should become a separate nation. It is poor. It has a small population. It has little industry. It could not defend itself against the stronger states that surround it.

The Arabs know all this. They simply want to see this territory free of Israeli soldiers so that it could be used as a base from which to launch attacks against Israel.

Is there proof that the Arabs don't believe the West Bank should be an independent country? Yes!

The Arabs captured this territory during the Israeli War of Independence. Did they give it independence? No. They made it part of the Kingdom of Jordan—an oppressed part. All real power was kept east of the Jordan River. The West Bank remained poor and undeveloped.

All rights of government, all industry, all improved standards of living, all political rights that the West Bank Arabs now enjoy have come since the Israelis freed them from Arab rule.

**Who Are the Palestinians?** "Only when the Palestinians have a state of their own can there be peace in the Middle East." In one sentence the Arabs combine several lies.

First is the word "Palestinian." It should mean "someone who lived in Palestine." This would include all citizens of Jordan, since Jordan was part of Palestine before 1921. It would include the Jews who lived in cities like Hebron before the Arabs drove them out.

The Arabs have redefined the word to mean those Arabs who left Israel when the state was created, confident that the Arab armies would destroy it. When Israel survived, the Arabs who had left to help in the nation's destruction were homeless.

The other Arab nations, who were chasing out their Jewish citizens, refused to give homes to the Arab refugees. These poor people were forced to remain in refugee camps run by the United Nations and paid for largely by the United States. The Soviet Union did not contribute a penny to help the Arab poor, though it gave millions of dollars to Arab terrorists. The principal thing given the refugees was the name "Palestinians" and the idea that they could claim rights which they had never received from any Arab state.

**Palestinians Speak of Peace** Even if the Palestinian claims aren't quite just, shouldn't Israel yield in order to get peace?

That is just the question the Arabs want you to ask. See how well the Big Lie works?

This empty refugee camp tells the tragic story of the Palestinian refugees. During the War of Independence, many Palestinian Arabs fled into neighboring Arab countries. They were housed in temporary camps, like this one near Jericho in the West Bank, where they waited confidently for the Arab victory that would destroy Israel. But Israel survived, and the Arab governments left the refugees in the camp for almost 20 years. During the Six Day War of 1967, when Israel conquered the area from Jordan, the Palestinians fled once again, leaving an empty camp behind them.

The question you should ask is, "Would the Palestinians really make peace with Israel if they were given a state?"

Consider what they have done to their Arab brothers and sisters. Palestinian groups made so much trouble in Jordan that they were brutally expelled. They established bases in Lebanon, which until they came was properous and democratic. The Palestinians plunged the country into civil war. The government was left powerless, the economy collapsed.

This is how the Palestinians behave to other Arabs, who are supposed to be their friends. What do you think they would do to Israel, which they have sworn to destroy?

**Israel Sacrifices for Peace**　Israel is always told to give things up to make the Arabs more reasonable. Israel has already made huge sacrifices for peace. The most obvious is the Sinai Peninsula, which it took from Egypt in two wars—and returned each time that peace was promised. It was returned even though it meant closing Jewish settlements and giving up wells that supplied a large part of the oil Israel needed.

Still, the world tells Israel, "Not enough. Give the Golan Heights back to Syria."

When these mountains were in Arab hands, they were used by soldiers mainly to shoot down on peaceful Israeli farms in the Jordan Valley. The Golan is now being used both to protect Israel and to raise food.

"Give back the area you call Judea and Samaria, the so-called West Bank."

Jews had lived in this area for centuries until they were driven out by rioting Arabs. The cities are as sacred to Jews as to Arabs. Why should the Jews leave?

"Give back the Old City of Jerusalem."

According to the UN agreement of 1947, Jerusalem was to be an international city. The Arabs rejected and violated that agreement. They took the Old City, drove the Jews out, destroyed Jewish cemeteries, schools, and synagogues, and prevented Jews from visiting their holy sites. Today it is a free city, open to all religions. Why should it change?

**The Ache Continues**　Israel is in the right. The Arab states are using the Big Lie. The situation of the Israeli Arabs is far better than it was under Arab rule. It is far better than that of Jews still in Arab lands. The Jews trapped in Syria and Iraq are persecuted, mistreated, and not allowed to leave.

Arab states are rich and large, and have small populations. These countries could easily give homes to Arab refugees from Palestine, just as Israel gave homes to Jewish refugees from Arab lands.

And yet . . .

The Israeli conscience still aches. The Israeli looks into the face of an Arab child growing up in a refugee camp. A child who has never known a home, who is learning hate instead of love, who may be taught to throw a hand grenade before he is taught to read. The Israeli thinks of the concentration camps and the Displaced Person camps.

Many Palestinians feel that they deserve a state of their own. At this demonstration masked young men wave their national flag.

The Druse are a major ethnic group in Israel. Although they speak Arabic and have a religion based on Islam, they do not identify with the Palestinians. They cooperate with the Israeli government and even serve in the army. Here a Druse officer, a specialist in community relations for the Israeli army, meets with local Palestinians in a town near Gaza.

So while the Arab nations use that child for propaganda purposes instead of giving him a decent place to live, Israel feels the pain and asks: "Is there something more that we can do for peace?"

## SUMMARY

Rather than make peace, the Arab states have worked in the United Nations and elsewhere to condemn Israel. They have used the Nazi "Big Lie" technique, claiming that Israel has cheated Arabs of all sorts of rights. In fact, Arabs have had more rights under Israeli rule than under Arab rule. Israel has made great sacrifices for peace, while Arabs have left their brothers and sisters in miserable refugee camps for propaganda purposes. The Israelis recognize the suffering that has taken place, and are eager for meaningful ways to improve the situation.

Chapter Eighteen

# The Magic Mirror

**W**e have traced the story of Israel from the earthquake that created the Jordan River Valley up to the political earthquakes of our own day.

But what is it like to be in Israel?

Almost all visitors to Israel use the same words to describe their experience: "Wonderful!" "Unforgettable!" "Beautiful!"

"Yes," you say, "but what is it really like?"

**Bursting With Energy**   Israel is a land that seems to be bursting with energy. So much is new! A tiny town like Ashdod now has a vital international port. The ancient city of Beersheva, at the northern edge of the Negev wilderness, has grown from 3000 inhabitants to the home of 150,000. Dozens of new kibbutzim, settlements, and even whole cities have sprung up.

Even the hills seem to breathe excitement. On one side you may see mature trees, near them a grove of younger trees, and nearby a grove of young seedlings, just planted by the Jewish National Fund and ready to grow in the rebuilt soil.

**A Feeling of Achievement**   There is a feeling of remarkable achievement. A land whose people were mostly refugees now has some of the most advanced technical laboratories and manufacturing plants in the world. Israeli scientists do research for the United States government and American corporations. Israel has produced startling breakthroughs in medical technology and computers.

Israel has been forced to be successful in producing military equipment and in methods of warfare. In these areas, too, it has helped the United States.

**Beauty and Learning**   Israel is a land of outstanding schools and universities, like the Hebrew University in Jerusalem. It has

Rooftop solar panels heat water for these Israeli homes. Israel is a world leader in solar-heating technology.

some of the world's most interesting museums. It has opera and theatre, and many orchestras. In fact, it is the only country that had an orchestra before it had a government! The Israel Philharmonic was founded under the name "Palestine Orchestra" in 1936.

Often Israel has managed to combine beauty and practicality. An exceptionally handsome building in Haifa harbor turns out to be a wonderfully designed grain silo.

Israel seems to have every kind of art and craft. Traditional Yemenite jewelry, lovely glasswork, pottery, and modern paintings are available to buy, or to admire in galleries and museums.

**Old and New**   Israel is a land that combines the old and the new. No other land has so many important historical sites in such a small area. Not far from a Crusader ruin may be a lovely beach equipped for modern water sports. You visit a 3000-year-old Canaanite altar by traveling in an air-conditioned bus.

The IBM Tower. Tel Aviv's residents are proud of their city's superb modern architecture.

The ancient past has left many signs in present-day Israel. These excavations, close to the Western Wall, have revealed the smooth paving stones of a wide avenue. On a typical morning 2000 years ago, this road was crowded with Roman soldiers, Jerusalem shopkeepers, and worshippers on their way to the great Temple.

The town of Caesaria was a capital city in Roman times. Now that it has been excavated, the outdoor amphitheatre has been rebuilt and is a beautiful site for concerts.

**The Magic Mirror**   Israel is a place of wonderful things to see, but it is also like a mirror. When you visit the land of Israel you begin to see yourself—often in a new way.

Jerusalem, capital of Israel and spiritual center of Jewish people everywhere, is one of the world's most fascinating cities.

Christians look at this mirror and find their faith deepened as they visit the place where (according to Christian belief) God took human form and walked on earth.

Muslims find their faith deepened by worshipping at the sacred shrine where (according to Islam) Muhammad rose to heaven.

Jews find themselves believing in miracles, for the very existence of a Jewish state seems to be a miracle. They remember the words of God to Abraham:

I give the land you sojourn in to you and your offspring to come . . . as an everlasting possession.

(Genesis 17:8)

And they see that the promise has come true.

**On a Personal Note**   I remember the first time I was in the port city of Jaffa. The waters of the Mediterranean Sea lapped against the shore, as they have for so many centuries. It didn't seem very special until my father said, "Do you realize that this is the town from which Jonah's boat set sail?"

I remember when I visited the country in 1961, and took photographs through the barbed wire that separated Israel from Jordan. The barbed wire is gone now, and I have visited those sites which Jews could not enter until after the Six Day War.

I think of sitting in the synagogue on top of Masada. The heat is so terrible that any effort is exhausting. Down the sides of the mountain I can clearly see the remains of the Roman camp, and try to imagine living on the top of that rock, year after year, waiting for the Romans to attack. And I think of the Israeli pledge —"Masada shall never fall again."

**Jerusalem**   My mind always comes back to my first approach to the Old City of Jerusalem. Our bus was driving through the barren but beautiful hills. Then, in the distance, I could see the top of a tower. Could that be Jerusalem? The tower hid behind a hill. The bus puffed on, and there it was. Unmistakable. The City of David. All the pictures I had ever seen suddenly came to life before me. And our tour guide stopped the bus, and asked us all to join in the ancient prayer he always spoke when he was about to reenter the sacred city:

*Baruch atta adonai, elohenu melech haolam, shehecheyanu, v'keyimanu, v'higeeyanu laz'man hazeh*

Blessed art Thou, O Lord our God, King of the Universe, who has given us life, sustained us, and brought us to this season.

**Or . . .**   Suddenly that memory is pushed aside by some very simple things.

The bus driver who knew how to speak seven languages . . .

The bomb shelter for the children in a kibbutz . . .

The first sight of a billboard advertising an American product—in Hebrew . . .

The Jewish star flying over a Jewish state . . .

Planting a tree with my own hands in the ancient soil . . .

Having to leave.

**Time to Leave**   For finally it was time to leave. It was time for each trip to end, just as it is time for this book to end.

Yet when you have visited Israel, you find that your appetite has only been whetted. Instead of having enough, you want to return. There is so much more to see, to experience.

I hope that you will have a chance to visit Israel. In the meantime, I hope this book will stimulate your appetite for other books about Israel. There is so much more to read, so many more beautiful pictures to see, so much more to learn.

**At Parting** There are two ways to say "Goodbye" in Hebrew.

*L'hitraot* really means "Until we see each other again." And as you say "Goodbye" to Israel, or to a book about Israel, *l'hitraot* is a good word to use.

The other word is *Shalom.* And that is an even better word to use, since it contains the wish that every Israeli, every Jew, and every person of good will has for the land of Israel.

*Shalom* means "Peace."

"L'hitraot!"

# Index

# PHOTO CREDITS